THE MAYFLOWER PILGRIMS

BY
EDMUND JANES CARPENTER

· A PUBLICATION OF ·

Christian Liberty Press

502 West Euclid Avenue, Arlington Heights, Illinois 60004

PRESENT PUBLISHER'S PREFACE

We are honored to bring you a classic textbook. This particular textbook is designed to improve a student's reading skills and comprehension.

To be able to read is to have the foundation for all subsequent education. The child whose reading training is deficient grows up to become the child who is frustrated, in despair, and soon to join the ranks of the drop-outs, the pushed-outs, the unemployed and the unemployable.

Millions of Americans are handicapped in their reading skills. The "look-say" method of teaching, rather than the older "phonics" technique, has resulted in a generation of functional illiterates. It has been revealed that the U.S. literacy rate has dropped to the level of Burma and Albania and is rapidly approaching that of Zambia.

Not only is the method of teaching reading of vital importance, but also the literary quality of the reading material. So much of what passes for "modern" readers in education today is nothing more than pablum that stresses "social adjustment".

The Bible says we are to do "all for the glory of God" (I Corinthians 10:31). Reading for God's glory necessitates reading material that draws attention to Him and His truth, that reflects His majesty, and that meets the standards of the Holy Scriptures. What this means is that we should take any reading selection to Philippians 4:8 and ask these simple questions: "Is it true? Is it noble? Is it right? Is it pure? Is it lovely? Is it admirable? Is it excellent? Is it praiseworthy?"

As we look at the American readers of days gone by we find that the Biblical standard was followed. Such readers featured the finest British and American authors who emphasized God, morality, the wonders of creation, and respect for one's country.

It is our prayer that this series will give to the reader the joy that is to be associated with "good reading", and that the knowledge imparted will help "make wise the simple" (Psalm 19:7).

Michael J. McHugh
Curriculum Director

Dr. Paul D. Lindstrom
Superintendent of Schools

CONTENTS

LIST OF ILLUSTRATIONS

I

WHO WERE THE PILGRIMS?

WHO were the Pilgrims? Whence did they come? Why did they emigrate to the inhospitable shores of New England? What were their distinctive religious opinions? These are queries often asked and once impossible to answer. The people of New England have never been without the knowledge that Governor William Bradford left, at his death, a manuscript book of the history of the Colony of Plymouth. This book was quoted by the early writers of our country. The Plymouth records contain references to or extracts from this manuscript. Thomas Prince, Cotton Mather, Hubbard, the early New England historian, and Governor Hutchinson all allude to it, or quote from it. It was in the possession of the last named writer as late as the year 1767, when the second volume of his history was written. But from that time onward, for nearly one hundred years, it disappeared from the knowledge of Americans.

In the year 1855, an historical writer and investigator, who was engaged in perusing a copy of Bishop Wilberforce's History of the Protestant Episcopal Church in America, found in it certain passages which seemed to him familiar. They were stated by the author to be quotations from an ancient manuscript history in the library of the Bishop of London at Fulham Palace. Surely these extracts were marvelously similar to certain quotations from the long-lost Bradford manuscript, as contained in the works of the early New England writers. The clew was slight, but it sufficed. An English antiquary and scholar was asked to examine the manuscript said to be in the library at Fulham Palace. This he did with the most agreeable results. It was, indeed, the long-missing manuscript. It was copied, at the request of the Massachusetts Historical Society, and soon after published by them. In the year 1897 the original volume, by order of the English ecclesiastical authorities, was returned to Massachusetts and is now sacredly preserved in the State House at Boston and has been published at the expense of the State.

WHO WERE THE PILGRIMS?

The late Senator Hoar, of Massachusetts, alluded to this book as "the most precious manuscript on earth, unless we could recover one of the four Gospels as it came in the beginning from the pen of the evangelist." Certainly, its extraordinary discovery served to reveal to the world of to-day some of the hidden things of earth. We learned that the Pilgrims were of the wing of English nonconformists, known variously, in their day, as Brownists, Independents, or Separatists. For the purposes of this inquiry the name of Separatists is preferred; for Robert Browne, perhaps the earliest leader of Separatism, after a few years of leadership became an apostate to the faith and returned to the fold of the English church. The name of "Brownist," indeed, was never especially relished by the members of this sect, and after Browne's apostasy it was repudiated, being used by adherents of the English Church as a term of reproach. Indeed, "Brownism" was regarded in the England of the seventeenth century as an offense against the law of the land.

A broad distinction must at the outset be drawn between the two great nonconformist wings of the English Established Church of that period—the Puritans and the Separatists. The sixteenth century was an era of transition, a period in which the human mind, dimly looking into the mists of the future, was girding and preparing itself for a struggle which was to end, long years after, in the establishment of new thoughts, new principles, a broader life and a more thorough recognition of human rights and duties. The struggle for freedom in religion cannot be said to have had its source wholly in the movement which alike affected religious thought and human civilization, and which we know as the Reformation. It had its origin in the human heart and soul two centuries before Luther nailed his ninety-five theses to the door of the Church of All Saints at Wittenberg. Even in the seventh century the claim of the Bishop of Rome to the headship of the Christian world was but grudgingly acknowledged in England. In the year 702, when a great synod was held at Austerfield, King Alfred and the bishops of the realm defied the edict of the pope, deposed Wilfred, Bishop of York, and practically declared the independence of England of the control of the bishop of Rome. Following the Reformation in Germany, "the church and people of England," says Dr. Lindsay,[1] "broke away from the mediæval papal ecclesiastical system in a manner so exceptional that the rupture had not very much in common with the contemporary movements in France and Germany. Henry VIII destroyed the papal supremacy, spiritual and temporal, within the land which he governed; he cut the bands which united the Church of England with the great Western Church ruled over by the bishop of Rome; he built up what may be called a kingly papacy on the ruins of the jurisdiction of the pope. His starting point was a quarrel with the pope, who refused to divorce him from Catharine of Aragon."

"It would be a mistake, however," continues this historian, "to think that Henry's eagerness to be divorced from Catharine accounts for the English Reformation. There was a good deal of *heresy,* so called, in England long before Luther's voice had been heard in Germany." Henry, to effect his purpose, merely took advantage of a condition which existed, and had existed for centuries, in his realm. And he having established himself as the head of the church in England, his successors saw,

---

[1] Lindsay: History of the Reformation, II. 315sqq.

as they believed, a necessity for maintaining the worship of that church, as a means of maintaining at the same time their own claims to the throne.

King Henry died, and after the brief reign of the boy king, Edward, Mary, the daughter of the Spanish princess Catharine, came to the throne. The horrors of the Inquisition, then raging furiously in Spain, had their reflex in the like tragedies of her short and inglorious reign.

The story of the reign of Mary Tudor, to whom a hard and well-deserved fate has given the title of "Bloody Mary," has so often been told that it is unnecessary to do more than to allude to it here. It was Mary's great desire to bring back the English Church and nation to obedience to Rome; but Queen Mary died and her persecutions for the cause of the Church of Rome ceased, while the church bells rang merrily out upon the English air. The fires of Smithfield died away and for a time it seemed to the people of England that religion and statecraft need not necessarily be bound together. The great Puritan movement arose, which had for its object the purification of the English Church from the abuses into which it had fallen, and from the last trace of Romanism. The severity of Elizabeth for a time extended no farther than to the putting of a bishop in jail because he preferred to dispense with the vestments which had been the church's heritage from Rome. But the Puritans, although following the teachings of Calvin, had no thought of separation from the English Church. They objected to kneeling to receive the holy communion, as being an act of adoration of the Real Presence; and for a while, in the English churches, some who thus objected were suffered to receive it standing or sitting. Hence has come down to Methodists the provision of the Discipline, that they who object to receiving the communion kneeling may receive it standing or sitting.

But, broken loose from the bonds of Rome, the people of England found themselves embarked, as it were, on an unknown sea of religious thought and in a condition of unrest and transition. The separation from Rome, the establishment of the English Church apart from papal control, the rise even of Puritanism, failed to satisfy some who were looking, perhaps dimly, forward to a new life, in which all bonds of conventionalism should be broken away. Even in the days of Edward the Sixth and of Mary Tudor there were many secret gatherings by night for prayer and religious converse, among those who saw that true righteousness had not its dwelling place in mere forms and ceremonies. Mary found her martyrs among some of these. And Elizabeth, far more beneficent than Mary, saw many reasons why the English Establishment should be maintained; for she was the daughter of Anne Boleyn, and through its maintenance were upheld the validity of the divorce of Catharine, her own legitimacy, and the security of her throne. When, therefore, a congregation was discovered engaged in their secret and interdicted worship, apart from the ceremonies of the Establishment, she felt no hesitation in thrusting the participants into prison. For these were of the secret sect of Separatists, who dared to obey their own consciences, as the voice of God. Five of these, who wrote and distributed tracts disseminating what Elizabeth regarded as the treasonable doctrines of the Separatists, found their way to the scaffold. These were John Copping and Elias Thacker, who were hanged in 1583, and John Greenwood, Henry Barrowe, and John

Penry, who followed them to the scaffold ten years later. But presently Elizabeth's conscience pricked her and she exclaimed, "Shall we put the servants of God to death?"

But after Elizabeth came James, who declared, "I will make them conform or I will harry them out of the land." And this he continued to do, some fleeing to Germany, others to Holland, until he found that these exiles were flooding England with heretical tracts, from their vantage grounds across the sea, and then he forbade their emigration.

An examination of the recovered manuscript of Governor Bradford revealed the fact that the Pilgrims were of the company of religionists called Separatists and that they had their origin in "sundrie townes and villages, some in Nottinghamshire, some of Lincolnshire, and some of Yorkshire, where they border nearest together." The map revealed this cluster of little English villages called Scrooby, Austerfield, and Gainsborough, charming little hamlets, of which more later. Our concern is just now with these people themselves, who and what they were and by what means they came in conflict with the English authorities and were constrained to flee from their native country. It was during the later years of the reign of Elizabeth that a little band of religionists united themselves together in this little cluster of English villages. "So many of these professors," says Bradford, "as saw the evil of these things in these parts, and whose hearts the Lord had touched with heavenly zeal for His truth, they shook off this yoke of antichristian bondage and as the Lord's free people joined themselves (by a covenant of the Lord) into a church estate, in the fellowship of the Gospel, to walk in all His ways, made known, or to be made known unto them, according to their best endeavors, whatever it should cost them, the Lord assisting them." This was the origin and foundation of the Pilgrim Church of Plymouth, which was carried from Scrooby over the seas to Amsterdam, thence to Leyden, and thence to the bleak shores of New England.

They who study carefully the various contending conditions abroad in English life at this time will presently perceive that the struggle for freedom in religious thought and practice was quadrangular. First, stood the old Church of Rome, contending for absolutism for her pope and clergy. Next, the

Church of England, denying the authority of the pope, either in religious or in civil affairs, although for a while retaining many of the ceremonials and dogmas of the Church of Rome. Thirdly, the great Puritan wing of the English Church, denying Roman dogmas, detesting the Roman vestments and ceremonials, and demanding a greater simplicity in faith and worship. Lastly arose the body of Separatists, Independents, or Brownists, as they were variously termed, who, in common with the Puritans, accepted the tenets of Calvin, but, despairing of a reformation in doctrine and mode of worship in the English Church, called upon the faithful to separate wholly from the Establishment and to form independent bodies or churches for worship in faith and simplicity. It was this last named sect, or faction, to which our Pilgrim Fathers belonged.

No one knows by what means an interest in Separatism, or Brownism, reached the little cluster of English villages which have been named. We find, however, at the beginning of our story, these little villages imbued with these doctrines and the people cautiously and secretly gathering together, on each succeeding Lord's Day, for prayer and religious conversation. It is believed, although not positively established, that the place of meeting in Scrooby village was the hayloft of the stable connected with an ancient mansion, once occupied as the manor house of the bishop, but at that time a station on the great royal post road, from London northward to Edinburgh. Every movement, social, political, or religious, has necessarily its leaders. This band of faithful ones found its leaders in William Brewster, who later became Elder Brewster of the Pilgrim Church, and a much younger man, William Bradford by name, in later years known as Governor Bradford of Plymouth Plantation, and the historian of the movement so humbly begun, but so broad in its results.

An English nonconformist clergyman, Dr. John Brown, who has been a profound student of Pilgrim life and history, tells us that but for the execution of Mary, Queen of Scots, there would have been no Elder Brewster and no Pilgrim Church in Scrooby, in Leyden, or in Plymouth, with all the far-reaching results of its establishment.[1] This remarkable statement is thus explained. William Brewster,

---

[1] Brown: The Pilgrim Fathers of New England, p. 58.

the great leader of the movement, in his young manhood was a secretary to William Davison, who was an under secretary of state to Queen Elizabeth. The queen's duplicity toward Davison is a matter of history well remembered. She greatly desired the death of her cousin Mary, the Scottish queen, then a prisoner at Fotheringay Castle, but yet she hesitated to take the extreme step of ordering her execution. She would doubtless willingly have laid the responsibility upon the shoulders of Cecil, Lord Burghley, but he was too wily to be caught in the meshes of the queen's net. Then she signed Mary's death warrant and gave it to Davison, to be forwarded to Fotheringay. When the news came of Mary's death, the queen affected great indignation, accused Davison of having exceeded his instructions, and removed him from office. With Davison's fall, of course, fell Brewster, and, banished from the royal court, he returned to his home in the little village of Scrooby, where his father was the keeper of the royal post station, to which place he succeeded at his father's death.

Where William Brewster came in touch with the Separatist movement, of which Browne was then the chief exponent, has never been learned. But after his return to Scrooby he became interested in this religious reform, of which he later became the shining light.

The followers of Brewster were for the most part a humble folk. Brewster himself and his younger coadjutor, Bradford, were university-bred men; but the majority of their followers were husbandmen in the fields, or keepers of flocks in the villages and surrounding country in which they lived.

These, then, were the people whom history knows as the Pilgrims of New England, whose coming to our shores, three hundred years ago, was the true beginning of Christian civilization, as well as of democratic government, in our country.

II

THE PILGRIM REGION IN ENGLAND

AS we have seen, the region whence the Pilgrims came was a cluster of small villages in the north of England, at the point where Yorkshire, Nottinghamshire, and Lincolnshire join. This whole region, it is said, was once lowland, composed chiefly of marshes and swamps, at times overflowed by extraordinary tides from the North Sea.[1] Perhaps the best known of the poems of Jean Ingelow, it is remembered, is descriptive of one of these high tides on the coast of Lincolnshire. Centuries ago, however, cunning engineers, mainly Dutchmen, by a system of ditching, diking, and draining converted this swampy country into a region dry and fertile, beautiful for situation, covered with smiling gardens and fields of waving grain. Of the scores and perhaps hundreds of Americans who yearly make

---

[1] Griffis: The Pilgrims in Their Three Homes, p. 14.

their pilgrimage to the Pilgrim shrine at Scrooby, the major portion tell us that the most pleasing approach to the ancient and historic hamlet is on foot from the nearby town of Bawtry, situated about a mile to the northward of the village. Indeed, Bawtry is about equally distant from the villages of Scrooby and Austerfield, both famed in Pilgrim annals. The region lies on a line of railway, distant about one hundred and fifty miles north of London.

The walk from Bawtry to Scrooby is through one of the most lovely as well as most interesting regions in all England. The walk is by no means long and wearisome, for, while the attention of the traveler is taken by the fields, the meadows, and the winding waters of the stream where unite the Idle and the Ryton, the graceful spire of the church at Scrooby breaks upon the sight, through the sweeping branches of the great elms which arch the road. Scrooby is a tiny hamlet of scarcely more than two hundred souls. Austerfield, though a somewhat larger village, still has a population of less than four hundred. There is no reason to believe that these villages were larger in the Pilgrim time than to-day, and one of the mysteries which attach to Pilgrim history is by what means so important a religious movement could have had its origin in a community so thinly settled as this. The village of Scrooby, however, was situated on the Great North Road, which in the sixteenth century was the main highway leading from London to Edinburgh. Despite its small size and population, Scrooby was in those days a place of considerable importance. Here was a manor of the Archbishop of York, surrounded by an ancient moat and supporting a great manor house or mansion. In Pilgrim days this manor house, although still the property of the see of York, was used as a station of the great royal post road. Let it not be forgotten that in 1514, Wolsey, afterward the great cardinal, was the Archbishop of York. A few years later, Wolsey, who had been high in the favor of King Henry VIII, fell from his lofty estate, at the mandate of Anne Boleyn, and, banished from the royal presence, returned to his diocese, took up his residence at the manor house in Scrooby, and here he passed many of his later days.

This circumstance alone, had it no other claims, would readily place the little hamlet of

Scrooby in the list of historic places. But there are other things which must serve to add to its fame. In June, 1503, Margaret, daughter of King Henry VII—through whom, later, the Stuart sovereigns gained their right to the English throne—was married to King James IV of Scotland. On her wedding journey to her new home her way led through Scrooby, and here at the manor house she passed a night. Just one hundred years later Robert Carey, cousin of Queen Elizabeth, who lay dead at Richmond, rode stormily through the night, over the Great North Road, and through Scrooby, to carry to the grandson of Margaret the intelligence of the death of the queen of England and of his own accession to the English throne. King Henry VIII passed a night at the manor house in 1541. As we have already learned, it was in the manor house at Scrooby where dwelt the father of William Brewster, then the keeper of the royal post at this station on the Great North Road. Here, after the fall of Davison, Queen Elizabeth's secretary, young Brewster returned and became an assistant to his father. After the death of the latter, young Brewster succeeded to his position as keeper of the post. Here he became the leader of the religious movement which later resulted in the Pilgrim migration and the final settlement at Plymouth.

The old manor house, as it was in Brewster's day, is no longer standing. It is easy, however, to trace the line of its foundations, through the meadow which now covers the place; and a much smaller, but still ancient, dwelling covers a portion of the site. An archway, long since bricked up, shows the former entrance to some portion of the old mansion and a stable near by was evidently built of some of the materials of the old manor house, for overhead are certain curiously carved oak beams, once portions of the roof of some lordly hall.

Austerfield, lying two miles north of Scrooby, with the village of Bawtry midway between the two hamlets, was the home of William Bradford, afterward governor of Plymouth. Here, in the little Church of Saint Helen, is to-day to be seen the baptismal record of the little child; and not far away stands the unpretentious stone cottage in which the future governor was born. Austerfield, as well as Scrooby, is entitled to its historic fame. Here in the year 702, as we have before seen, was held the great ecclesiastical synod, which was in reality a struggle of the churches in England against the assumed supremacy of the bishop of Rome. The synod took the form of a hearing of a protest of Wilfrid, Bishop of York, concerning the proper date for the celebration of Easter. The English churches had adopted one calendar for computation; the pope employed another. Wilfrid, a warm advocate of papal supremacy, laid the matter before the bishop of Rome, and, of course, was sustained. King Egfrid deposed Wilfrid from his bishopric and the synod sustained his action—the first struggle in England against the claims of papal Rome.

The third of the Pilgrim villages is Gainsborough, lying some ten miles east of Scrooby and Austerfield, and thus forming the apex of a triangle. It was at Gainsborough, indeed, that the Separatist movement in this region may perhaps be said to have had its inception; for there in 1602 was formed, secretly of course, the formal church of the new faith, of which both Brewster and Bradford were original members. In this town, on the banks of the River Trent, King Alfred was married, and here Canute was proclaimed King of England. Here in the old hall King Henry VIII once held court when he came to Yorkshire in 1541 to receive the submission of a faction of revolting subjects. Hither came, every Sunday, on foot from Scrooby and Austerfield, Bradford and Brewster and others of the faithful brethren, to join in worship with them of Gainsborough and listen to the preaching of the pastor, John Smyth.

The region about this Pilgrim country is of unusual interest. Not far distant is Epworth, the shrine of Methodism throughout the world, the birthplace of John and Charles Wesley. Within easy distance is Sherwood Forest, renowned for centuries past as the scene of the exploits of Robin Hood and his band of kindly outlaws, who waylaid and robbed the wealthy and distributed the spoils to the poor. Who does not remember the ancient tale of Robin Hood and Friar Tuck, Little John, Scarlet, and Maid Marian, so ancient that its author's name is lost in the mists of antiquity? In this region too Scott laid the scene of Ivanhoe, and Kingsley his story of Hereward the Wake. Gainsborough too is the "St. Oggs" of George Eliot's novel The Mill on the Floss. The River

Trent, which flows here, is the "Floss" and the "Dorlcote Mill" still stands below the town. And if we turn again from literature to history, we find, not far from Scrooby and Austerfield, the walls of Fotheringay Castle, where for eighteen years Mary, Queen of Scots, was held a prisoner of state and where she met her death at the hands of the executioners.

Such was the region in which the great Pilgrim movement had its rise. It must not be understood that this region was necessarily the center of the entire Separatist movement of which the Scrooby congregation was but a part. Robert Browne, usually regarded as the originator of the movement for separation, probably never visited Scrooby. As already suggested, by what means the sentiment became rife in this far-away cluster of villages in the north of England is a mystery. But there was perhaps no portion of England at that day to which this movement did not penetrate. Until the authorities discovered, probably through an informer, that Brewster and a company at Scrooby were of the pernicious sect of Brownists, the village of Bury Saint Edmunds, in West Suffolk, was believed to be the place chiefly infested with this heresy; and there were undoubtedly many secret meetings of Separatists held in London itself. Since Scrooby was on the main highway from London to Edinburgh, it is not improbable that some traveler, passing a night at the old manor house, brought this phase of the gospel to the ears of Brewster, who spread the story to others. We know too that Brewster, while in the employ of Davison, on one occasion accompanied his master upon a special embassy to Holland, then the refuge of many whose religious convictions had led them to flee from England.

At all events, in Scrooby the movement for Separatism had taken such firm root that its leaders and adherents perhaps grew less wary in their movements. The weekly foot journey of ten miles to Gainsborough and return had become too wearisome for hard working people to endure and a division had occurred, a separate church being formed in Scrooby, of which Brewster was the leader. Bradford, finding it far more convenient to walk from Austerfield, through Bawtry, to Scrooby, every Sunday, than to undertake the twenty-mile journey to Gainsborough and return, joined his fortunes with those of Brewster. Frequent meetings for prayer and religious converse were held, probably in the hayloft of the stable of the manor house, until there came a day of discovery. Brewster, who had been absent, probably in London upon government concerns, returned home to find that a considerable company of the faithful, including his own wife, had been arrested and lodged in jail. Brewster fortunately escaped and went into hiding. Bradford does not seem, at this time, to have been known openly as a Brownist, and he also escaped the clutches of the law.

But this discovery brought to the leaders the stern alternative of flight from the country or the abandonment of their faith. To their minds there was no alternative; apostasy was not for a moment to be considered. Nothing was left but flight. The "lock-up" in this tiny village was probably inadequate for the permanent detention of the arrested ones and they were soon set at liberty. The story of the flight to Holland must be told in another chapter.

III

THE FLIGHT TO HOLLAND

AS we have already learned, the Separatist Church at Gainsborough was formed in 1602. That at Scrooby was formed in 1606. The formation was simple. The friends were gathered together, probably in the hayloft of the stable adjacent to the manor house. We are told that "there was first one stood up and made a covenant, and then another, and these two joined together, and so a third, and these became a church." Now comes into the story one Richard Clyfton, described by Bradford as "a grave and revered preacher, who by his pains and diligence had done much good and under God had been the means of the conversion of many." Mr. Clyfton at the beginning of our story was the rector of the English Church at Babworth, a village some eight miles south of Scrooby. The cause of the Separatists, by the execution of Greenwood and Barrowe had received a severe check; but it was just at this period of discouragement that the Scrooby church was formed.

Richard Clyfton had been educated at Cambridge, as had also Brewster. He was some years older than Brewster, for he was born in 1553, while Brewster's natal year was 1566. He had been the rector of Babworth for sixteen years when he cast in his lot with the Scrooby brethren. There had been for some years serious scandals, involving many of the English Church clergy in this region. Lord Burghley, the premier of Elizabeth, is quoted as having openly accused the Bishop of Lichfield of having "made seventy ministers in one day for money, some tailors, some shoemakers, and other craftsmen." There are even records of English "gentlemen," who had church "livings" at their disposal, having procured the appointment of their stewards or coachmen to the vacancies, that the emoluments of the positions might be turned into their own treasuries. Such a man as Clyfton could not remain content with such conditions in the church, and he had long been recognized as a Puritan and reformer. The exact date at which he broke with the English Church is not fixed, but it was not far from the opening year of the seventeenth century. How he occupied himself from this time until the formation of the church at Scrooby is uncertain, but the fact is established that he became its first pastor. Associated with him as his assistant was the Rev. John Robinson, who joined his fortunes to those of the Scrooby brethren in 1604. He too was a Cambridge graduate. He was for a time in charge of a parish near Norwich, but lost this position by reason of his advanced views. Then came his separation from the English Church and his union with the Scrooby movement.

William Bradford, who must be mentioned in this connection—for Brewster, Clyfton, Bradford, and Robinson were the four great leaders of this movement—was led to take an interest in the Separatist idea mainly through the teachings of Clyfton at Babworth, ten miles distant from his home in Austerfield. He was a member of a family of English gentry, from whom he was estranged by reason of his course in religious affairs, doubtless being regarded by his relatives as erratic. He was more than twenty years younger than Brewster, and indeed was only a youth of seventeen when he first began to meet with the brethren at Scrooby. It was not until some years later, therefore, that he became a force among them. Brewster, Clyfton, and Robinson, especially the first two named, were men of some prominence in this region, and it is not surprising that their activity in the tiny hamlet of Scrooby soon attracted the attention of the authorities. The meetings of the church were held with great secrecy. Bradford says of Brewster that "after they were joyned together in communion he was a special stay and help to them. They ordinarily met at his house on the Lord's Day, which was a manor of the bishop's, and with great love he entertained them when they came, making provision for them to his great charge."

But little is known of the rank and file of the little congregation. It is certain that they were for the most part humble folk. Since this was an agricultural region, they were undoubtedly chiefly farmers, upon lands leased from the archbishop's holdings. None save the four leaders were probably educated, although all perhaps were able to write, for none of the signatures affixed to the Compact at Cape Cod were, so far as is known, signed with a cross. All were people sincere in their convictions and firm in their faith.

Scarcely a year had passed after the formation of the church at Scrooby when persecution fell upon them. Bradford says that they "could not long continue in any peaceable condition, but were hunted and persecuted on every side, so as their former afflictions were but as flea-bitings in comparison of those which now came upon them. For some were taken and clapt up in prison, others had their houses beset and watcht night and day and hardly escaped their hands; and the most were faine to flie and leave their howses and habitations and the means of their livelihood. Yet these and many other sharper things which afterward befel them were no other than they looked for and therefore were the better prepared to bear them, by the assistance of God's grace and spirit."

In the records of the ecclesiastical court at York is found ample corroboration of these statements of Bradford, concerning the persecution of the Scrooby people for cause of conscience. These records show that one "Gervase Neville of Scrowbie, one of the sect of Barrowists, or Brownists, holding and maintaining erroneous opinions and doctrines," was arrested upon a warrant issued to one William Blanchard, messenger, and confined in York Castle. On September 15, 1607, a warrant was issued for the apprehension of Richard Jackson and William Brewster for Brownism. The return upon the warrant certified that the officer had been unable to find the two culprits. There was good reason for this failure of the officers of the law to find and apprehend William Brewster, for at that very time he was doubtless in Boston, on the coast of Lincolnshire, endeavoring to obtain passage for himself and his neighbors to Holland. The wife of William Brewster had some weeks before this been arrested and confined in York Castle. The long arm of persecution was reaching out for him, and nothing seemed left but flight, if possible, to Holland, a country which, since the days of William the Silent, had been a refuge for the oppressed in the cause of religion. There was even then in Amsterdam a colony of English religious refugees, some from London, others from other parts of the kingdom. Indeed, it is probable, if not certain, that some of these refugees were from among their own neighbors at Gainsborough. Thither they therefore resolved to turn their faces.

A serious undertaking was this for these simple people, and to them it meant much. They must leave the places which they called home, where the greater number of them had been born. Wholly unaccustomed to travel, they must dispose of their household goods as best they might, abandon their means of livelihood, and with but little money, go forth across the sea, into a foreign land, where all were strangers and where a strange tongue was spoken. Not only this, but having reached that unknown land, they must without delay seek a new means of gaining a livelihood.

But it was a stern necessity which confronted them and a necessity full of tribulations and dangers. To leave the country without a license was forbidden by law, and the party knew that to obtain a license to emigrate for the cause of religion, would be impossible. Too many Separatists already were taking advantage of the freedom of the press in Holland and were sending over into England their schismatic writings. If they were to emigrate to this land of promise, it must be by stealth. From time to time attempts were made by small detached parties to obtain passage, but in every case they were detected and their persons and effects seized by officers of the law. The case had, however, become desperate, and Brewster, while the officer was seeking him to serve the warrant of arrest upon him, was bargaining with the captain of a vessel lying at the port of Boston to convey the entire Scrooby party across the sea. The captain affected to make a bargain for the passage of the party, but meanwhile was plotting for their betrayal.

It was in September, 1607, that the attempt at flight was made. It is probable that the men of the company made the journey from Scrooby to Boston in small parties, on foot and by night. The women and children, with such of their household goods as they could take with them, were conveyed by boat down the Trent and Humber to tidewater and so to Boston. All seemed to be progressing well. The party arrived at the coast by night and was taken in open boats to the vessel which was anchored off shore. But the officers of the law were in waiting, the party was arrested, robbed and maltreated, and taken back to Boston as prisoners. There were cells beneath

WHERE GOVERNOR WILLIAM BRADFORD LIVED IN PLYMOUTH

CELLS IN GUILD HALL, BOSTON, ENGLAND

the Guild Hall, and here were these male-
factors thrust, while they awaited the action
of the law for their crimes. The old building
and the cells in the basement are still to be seen.

Here, huddled together, these unhappy
people—men, women, and children—were confined for a time. The magistrates, having
strong Puritan sympathies, treated them as
courteously as possible, but were unable to
release them without an order from the Privy
Council at London; and there were no railway
trains, telegraphs, nor telephones in those
days. But it was impossible to keep these
women and children long in confinement and
they were presently released, a few of the leaders being detained in jail for a month or more.
It is probable that among these unfortunates
were Brewster, Clyfton, and Robinson, and
perhaps Bradford. How or when these obtained their liberty is unknown; but this failure, although discouraging, did not cause them
to desist from their purpose. A second attempt was made in the spring of 1608, and although accompanied by great difficulties, at
last proved successful. This time a bargain
was made with a Dutch captain. The journey
from Scrooby to the coast was accomplished

as before, the vessel lay off shore, and all seemed going well. But a delay was caused by a low tide, and when at length one boatload of the refugees had been put on board, a posse of civil officers and soldiers was seen in pursuit of the party still on shore. Some were on horseback, some on foot, and all armed with guns, clubs, and other weapons. The party which had been taken on board was composed chiefly of the men of the company. The women and children, with their goods, were in their boat, stranded by the low tide. These, then, fell into the hands of the roystering mob, which, under the cover of the law, descended upon them. The Dutch captain, alarmed for his own safety, hoisted sail and sailed away, leaving the most helpless portion of the company to the tender mercies of the mob.

The terror and distress of these poor women and children can scarcely be measured. Despite their tears and shrieks they were seized and mistreated, and hustled from one magistrate to another. But the men whose arrest the officers had chiefly sought had escaped their clutches and presently the women and children were released, after being stripped of their few possessions.

FLIGHT TO HOLLAND

How the party at length became reunited is not known. The vessel encountered a severe storm and narrowly escaped wreck; but the party at length reached Amsterdam, where, after a while, the women and children, in small detachments, joined them. And in the end," says Bradford, "notwithstanding all these storms of opposition, they all gatt over at length, some at one time and some at another and some in one place and some in another, and mett together again according to their desires with no small rejoicing."

IV

THE PILGRIMS IN HOLLAND

AS we have already seen, by no means all
of the sect of Separatists, Barrowists,
Independents, or Brownists—as they were
variously termed—were found among the
people of the Pilgrim region. In many parts
of England were these people found, especially in Norfolk, Essex, and the vicinity of
London. So great became the numbers of
these peculiar people—whose chief insistence
was upon an entire separation of church and
state—that in this region alone, as early as
1593, they numbered fully twenty thousand.
They had become too numerous either for
scaffold or prison. Previous to this time many
had been confined in the loathsome prisons of
England. Even down to the year 1834 the
prison system of England was one of the most
fearful scandals known to modern civilization.
It is to the credit of our mother country that,
but little more than eighty years ago, it
modeled a great reform upon the prison sys-

tems of New York and Pennsylvania. But in the sixteenth century to be immured in an English prison was a punishment far worse than death at the hands of the hangman.

In 1593, recognizing the rapid growth of the Separatist movement, the Parliament, which contained a large proportion of Puritan members, adopted a measure by which it was hoped that the country might be rid of the presence of this pestilent sect. It was enacted that any person above sixteen years of age who should absent himself from church without good cause for the space of one month, who should dissuade others from attendance, or who should write or say anything against the authority of the crown in ecclesiastical matters, or who should attend any unlawful conventicle, should be imprisoned without bail, and at the end of three months, if such should refuse to conform, should suffer banishment, with forfeiture of all his goods and chattels and the income of his real estate for life. Convicted persons refusing to leave the realm, or returning from banishment without leave, were to suffer death.

The enactment of this statute was in effect a general jail delivery for hundreds of poor people who were suffering confinement for the cause of conscience. No country was open to such refugees save the new republic across the North Sea, and thither they flocked in multitudes during the last ten years of the reign of Elizabeth. These people were poorly organized, the majority of them unlettered and wretchedly poor in worldly goods. They were largely fanatics, it is true, but they clung persistently to the doctrines of a separation of church and state and the support of ministers by voluntary contributions, and not by tithes —strange doctrines for their day, but in our time one of the foundation-stones of our great republic.

In Amsterdam was gathered the first church organization of these English refugees, who in 1611 put forth a Declaration of Faith, in which occurred this passage: "The magistrate is not to meddle with religion, or matters of conscience, nor compel men to this or that form of religion, because Christ is the King and Lawgiver of the church and conscience." It will be recalled that, when the English government found that the realm was being deluged with Separatist tracts from across the sea, the statute of banishment was abrogated and the emigration of English subjects, without leave, was forbidden.

We have seen, however, that the Scrooby Separatist church, which appears to have differed somewhat in doctrine from other churches of the sect, found no little difficulty in following their fellow religionists into Holland. As was natural, the objective point of the Pilgrims was Amsterdam. The Dutch ship which bore the first detachment made a landing at that port and thither drifted, in little companies and at various times, those of their church who had been left behind upon the shore. It must be remembered that both in their flight to and residence in Holland and in their emigration to America, the Scrooby Church maintained its individuality. At no time did this company become incorporated with the English Church established in Amsterdam, but continued its separate existence. Indeed, when the Scrooby congregation reached Amsterdam there were no fewer than seven religious bodies of English-speaking people in that city. Dr. W. E. Griffis, a writer upon Pilgrim history, and who has followed the footsteps of these people in Holland, tells us that of these bodies the Scotch Presby-

terian Church, formed in 1607, remains unto
this day, with an established house of worship.

"Being now come into the Low Countries,"
says Bradford, "they saw many goodly and
fortified cities, strongly walled and guarded
with troops of armed men. Also they heard a
strange and uncouth language, and beheld the
differente manners and customs of the people,
with their strange fashons and attires, all so
farre differing from that of their plaine countrie villages, wherein they were bred and had
so longe lived, as it seemed they were come into
a new world. But these were not the things
they much looked on, or long tooke up their
thoughts; for they had other work in hand and
another kind of warr to wage and maintaine.
For though they saw the faire and bewtifull
cities, flowing with abundance of all sorts of
welth and riches, yet it was not longe before
they saw the grime and grisly face of povertie
coming upon them like an armed man, with
whom they must bukle and incounter and
from whom they could not flye; but they were
armed with faith and patience against him and
all his encounters, and though they were sometimes foyled, yet by God's assistance they prevailed and got the victorie."

The Scrooby congregation remained about a year in Amsterdam. Bradford touches lightly upon the cause of the brevity of their stay at the city of their first residence in Holland. He tells us that Mr. John Smyth and his congregation—whom we remember as our old acquaintances at Gainsborough—were "already fallen into contention with the church that was there before them and no means they could use would doe any good to cure the same." The "flames of contention were like to breake out in the ancient church itself," he also tells us; and like the prudent man, who "foreseeth the evil and hideth himself," they determined to seek another home where they might have peace among themselves. "For these and other reasons," says Bradford, "they removed to Leyden."

Bradford goes no farther than this in explaining the causes which impelled the Scrooby church to leave Amsterdam. Later writers have, however, sought out some of these "other reasons." Besides the Gainsborough Church, led by the Rev. John Smyth, there was another English Separatist church nearby, led by the Rev. Francis Johnson. These two churches for a time lived in amity, but presently fell into dissensions over matters of church government. This was the main cause of the trouble which arose. But there was another matter which was the occasion of much heated discussion, accompanied by some heaviness of spirit. The wife of Pastor Johnson had been accustomed to more gay and fashionable attire than was favored by many of the more plainly dressed religionists. The brother of Mr. Johnson was especially scandalized at the too fashionable attire of his sister-in-law and broke forth into loud and long-continued denunciations of her "apparel unreformed." The quarrel was long and disagreeable. Sides were, of course, taken and an acrimonious controversy, always to be deprecated in a Christian church, dragged its weary length through many months, to the indefinite weariness and disgust of the Scrooby people, who above all things desired peace.

On February 12, 1609, therefore, Pastor Robinson addressed a letter to the authorities of the city of Leyden, asking permission, in behalf of himself and about one hundred parishioners, to come and reside in that city. The transcript of this letter is to be seen in the city records preserved at Leyden, with its indorsed reply that "the coming of the memorialists will be agreeable and welcome."

Here, then, in the beautiful city of Leyden, with its famous university and its heroic past, the wanderers in 1609 found a home. Their life here for some years was not eventful. Motley says that there "is not a trace left on the national records of the Netherlands of their protracted residence on the soil."[1] As a matter of course, their first care, on reaching the city, was to provide themselves, as best they could, with employment. As we have seen, their occupation in their old home in England was mainly agriculture. But Holland at that time seems to have been chiefly a pastoral and manufacturing country, so that little employment was offered in their own occupation. They turned, therefore, to manufactures. Leyden was then a great emporium for the manufacture of all kinds of woven goods. Some became, therefore, weavers of various fabrics in woolen, silk, and other materials, cotton, however, being in that day not much in use. Bradford is recorded, at the time of his marriage in 1613 to Dorothy May, as a fustian worker. Brewster busied himself as a teacher

[1] Motley: The Life of John Barneveld, II. 292.

of English to the sons of wealthy families; while Robinson was the leader of the flock, for Mr. Clyfton, being advanced in years, could not bring himself to make another removal and remained at Amsterdam.

To this peaceful community of English religionists others were attracted from the homeland, and now we find among them some names of men afterward notable in Pilgrim history. Of these newcomers one was Edward Winslow, one of the foremost in the foundation of the Plymouth Colony and thrice its governor. The portrait of Governor Winslow, preserved at Plymouth, is the only known portrait extant of any of the Pilgrim company. Others among these newcomers were Myles Standish, the military leader of the colony at Plymouth, and John Carver, the colony's first governor. Remarkably gentle and peaceable was this English colony in Leyden. Remarkable also were they for their probity. Although they were poor, yet so upright were they in their dealings, that the Leyden tradesmen had no hesitation in giving them credit and their confidence was never abused. "Such was their single-heartedness and sincere affection toward one another," says Bradford, "that they came as near the primitive pattern of the first churches as any other church of these later times has done, according to their rank and quality." The authorities of Leyden, on one occasion, in remonstrating with a Walloon congregation for their almost continued quarreling, said: "These English have lived among us ten years and yet never had any suit or accusation against any of them, but your quarrels are continual."

During their stay in Leyden a notable controversy, upon points of theology, was held among the professors at the University of Leyden. The death of the great theologian James Arminius, a professor in the university, had occurred in the very year in which the Pilgrims settled in Leyden. He was buried beneath Saint Peter's Church, where also, some years later, the English pastor, Mr. Robinson, was buried. A few years after his death—the exact date cannot be fixed—a fierce controversy arose in the university, in which Professor Episcopius vigorously defended the doctrines of Arminius, while Professor Polyander fought the fight of the Calvinists. Motley, in a footnote, says that he searched in vain for an account of this controversy other than that given by Bradford.[1] From his brief statement we gather that Professor Polyander appeared about to be worsted when the Calvinistic party resorted to Mr. Robinson, who had previously been admitted a member of the university, and begged him to enter the lists. This he somewhat reluctantly consented to do, and, according to the statement of Bradford, he so did "foyle this adversarie, as it caused many to praise God that the trueth had so famous victory." It is probable that the Arminian principle which Robinson chiefly combated was that of the supremacy of the state in religious matters, and not the theological tenet of free will , as opposed to the Calvinistic idea of predestination. We know that when the Pilgrims prepared to leave Leyden, Pastor Robinson, who remained behind, preached to them a farewell discourse, which discloses some trace of a Calvinistic spirit, but, as Motley says, "for loftiness of spirit and breadth of vision has hardly a parallel in that age of intolerance. He laid down the principle that criticism of the Scriptures had not been exhausted merely because it has been begun; that the hu-

---

[1] Motley: The Life of John Barneveld, II. 291.

man conscience was of too subtle a nature to be imprisoned forever in formulas, however ingeniously devised; that the religious reformation, begun a century ago, was not completed; and that the Creator had not necessarily concluded all His revelations to mankind." He thus charged them who were to go forth into the wilderness: "I charge you before God and His blessed angels that you follow me no farther than you have seen me follow the Lord Jesus Christ. If God reveal anything to you by any other instrument of His, be as ready to receive it as ever you were to receive any truth by my ministry; for I am verily persuaded that the Lord has more truth yet to break forth out of His Holy Word."[1] Whatever may have been the truth of which Bradford says that Robinson was so famous a champion, it is almost certain that this Separatist church in Leyden did not accept the doctrine of predestination, which had come to Amsterdam from Geneva and which had been there absorbed by the English Anabaptist congregations established in that city; and it is equally certain that this body of sincere reli-

---

[1] Ibid., II. 294.

gionists believed that in matters of salvation man's will was superior to God's divine will.

For twelve years this company remained at Leyden, when it seemed suitable that they should again remove and seek a new home. The reasons in detail for this removal must be reserved for a later chapter.

But before proceeding to rehearse the story of the voyage of the ship Mayflower, it will be useful to go back in our narrative for a few years and recall some features of the struggle for religious liberty in England, culminating, so far as our present story is concerned, in the establishment in Leyden, by William Brewster, of a secret press, from which emanated some books which greatly disturbed King James. Incidentally too it was the discovery of this secret publication house which in large measure served to hasten the departure of the Leyden Separatists and to make of them Pilgrims in search of a home in which they might worship God in the manner which their consciences prompted.

---

[1] Campbell: The Puritans in Holland, England and America, II. 247.

V

THE PILGRIM PRESS OF LEYDEN

THE struggle for liberty in religion in England was waged largely by the pamphleteers. Newspapers as we know them were quite unknown prior to 1588. Freedom of speech was a political dogma not yet so much as suggested. Secret meetings of religious independents, then, must be supplemented by the secret preparation and distribution of pamphlets, by means of which the sentiments of the reformers might be disseminated. We have already learned that in 1583 John Copping and Elias Thacker were put to death for having distributed certain of these pamphlets. This did not serve to deter those who felt impelled by conscience to promulgate these dangerous doctrines, although it doubtless impressed upon them the necessity of caution. It was not more than a year after the execution of these two men that an episode occurred which must be regarded as an important feature of this great struggle. This was the publication and secret distribution of a series of notable tracts, which appeared under the unusual signature of "Martin Marprelate."

The beginning of the especial controversy which called forth this remarkable series of tracts was the publication in 1584 of a small pamphlet entitled "A Learned Discourse of Ecclesiastical Government," in which, in a manner not especially objectionable to the authorities, the position of the Puritan reformers of the day was stated. No author's name appeared on the title page, but the pamphlet was confessedly printed and published by Robert Waldegrave, known to be a Puritan printer. This pamphlet attracted no little attention and evidently disturbed the officials of the Established Church and government, for Dr. John Bridges, Dean of Sarum, was appointed to make answer to it. This he did in a prodigious volume of some fourteen hundred quarto pages, which in its preparation occupied much of the Dean's time for the space of two years. This formidable book bore the title A Defense of the Government Established in the Church of England for Ecclesiastical Matters. Confessedly, this was a reply to the anonymous pamphlet popularly known as the Learned Discourse.

At intervals during the next two years tracts were published and circulated with the greatest secrecy, making reply to the "Defense" of Dr. Bridges, for it was evident that a matter which required such an elaborated defense must be worthy of careful and thorough discussion. In the year 1588, the year made notable and illustrious by the defeat and destruction of the Spanish Armada, appeared the first of the "Marprelate" tracts. This too was the period distinguished in English history by the great revival of letters—the period which produced Marlowe and Ben Jonson and Shakespeare. But it was a period, as well, in which the intolerant and cruel Archbishop Whitgift was casting into jail many good men and women, whose only offense had been the reading of the Bible in company with their friends, in the privacy of their own homes. It was a period in which spies of officials, political and ecclesiastical, were upon every hand and when the printing press was regarded as the most dangerous of forces, which must be hedged about with the most vigorous scrutiny. But the human mind cannot always remain confined and repressed, and the desire for freedom of thought is ever boundless in the human breast. In October, 1588, suddenly and with the utmost secrecy appeared the first of the series of seven tracts of "Martin Marprelate." The tract was in a vein wholly new. Hitherto the reformers had employed serious argumentative discourse; now the manner was changed to wit, sarcasm, and humorous irony. At once the attention of all classes was drawn to this new and original weapon of the nonconformists, and the bishops and other prelates became the object of the satirical laughter of the English people, upon all sides. A bad cause can reply to argumentation, can endure even a semblance of abuse; but it quails before ridicule and biting sarcasm.

Scarcely had subsided the laughter at the expense of the ecclesiastics, when a second pamphlet appeared. This was too much for Elizabeth's bishops well to endure, and Thomas Cooper, Bishop of Winchester, was incautious enough to issue a reply to it. This was exactly what "Martin Marprelate" desired; he had drawn the enemy's fire. A third tract soon appeared, which bore the title of a familiar London street cry; "Hay! Any work for the Cooper." Three other tracts of similar tenor followed and the ecclesiastical establishment of England broke into fury at the hidden attacks upon its dignity and supremacy. The story of the Marprelate tracts, the search for their author and their publisher; the accidental discovery at last of the printing press, through the stumbling of a workman engaged in moving a box of types—these were matters of common knowledge of the day. Years later it became known that the secret printing press, after producing one tract, would be removed by night in a cart, concealed beneath a load of turnips, and set up in some distant place, usually in the attic of some ardent but little-known dissenter. And it was revealed also, long years after the knowledge ceased to carry danger with it, that the printed pamphlets were conveyed from city to city for secret distribution, across the country by messengers clad in green, whose movements might thus less readily attract the attention of the curious.

The author of these dangerous tracts has never become absolutely known. With such secrecy was this propaganda conducted that even the printer and distributors themselves were ignorant of the identity of the writer. It is said that the "copy" for a new tract would sometimes be found by the printer, lying in his path in a woodland road. A vigorous search was instituted by the authorities for the discovery of the miscreants who thus dared to defy the authority of the ecclesiastics and to hold them up to ridicule. Many suspects were seized, some were put to the torture; one whose actual participation in the affair was not proved was hanged—the last execution in England for cause of conscience. The Marprelate press was seized and destroyed; but even after this occurrence one tract—the seventh—appeared, in which Martin Marprelate defied his enemies. But the publication of this series of tracts served to increase the zeal of both parties to the struggle in the cause of religious liberty, and although the Marprelate tracts ceased to appear, the publication of Puritan and Separatist literature was by no means, stayed. When vigorous espionage rendered it well-nigh impossible to produce such publications in England, the exiles who had fled from the persecution to the Continent flooded England with their writings, from their vantage points across the sea.

PILGRIM PRESS OF LEYDEN

William Brewster, we know, while at Scrooby, was denounced as a Brownist, was dogged by the sheriff's officers and escaped to his safe refuge in Holland. We have seen that he supported himself and his family in Leyden, mainly by giving instruction in English to the sons of wealthy families. But his sterling character would not brook inactivity and he longed for a part in the great struggle, which he knew was going on in the old homeland. We find him, therefore, in the autumn of 1616, setting up a printing press in Leyden, for the printing and publication of books in which the contentions of the English Separatists should be frankly stated. This is known to historians of the period as the Pilgrim Press of Leyden.

In this enterprise Brewster associated with himself one Thomas Brewer, like him an English exile, who was the silent partner in the affair, furnishing the funds for the purchase of the type and other equipment, but taking no other part in the work. They would appear to have had no printing press of their own, and it seems probable that after the type was set up and the forms made ready, some Dutch printer was employed to print off the sheets.

The types and cases were secreted in the attic of a dwelling house in Choir Alley, where the work of typesetting was performed.

The list of books printed and published by the Pilgrim Press of Leyden was not large. Two books, of a nature wholly unobjectionable to the English establishment, were confessedly issued by Brewster's press, for they bear his imprint. But when he began to print and issue books of a more dangerous character he became cautious and omitted his name and the place of printing from the title page. In 1617 and 1618 appeared in all four books of a non-contentious character, so far as the British government was concerned. The two already mentioned bore Brewster's imprint; the other two, although not bearing his name, unquestionably emanated from his press. In 1619 appeared a book entitled Perth Assembly, which attracted wide attention throughout England. King James the First, as we all know, was the son of Mary, Queen of Scots, and was himself a native of Scotland. In his early years he had been taken from the care and control of his Roman Catholic mother and had been brought up a Presbyterian. But when he came to the English throne, at the death of Elizabeth, and found the security of his throne practically dependent upon the maintenance of his position as the head of the English Church, he repudiated his Presbyterian affiliations and began a resolute attempt to destroy the Kirk of Scotland and force episcopacy upon the reluctant people. If we read English history further, we will find that his son, Charles the First, continued this attempt, with the result of precipitating the country into civil war and, at the last, of losing his own head. During the reign of James the General Assemblies of the Scottish Kirk were always struggles between the British king and the Scotch nation. In the Assembly which sat at Perth, in August, 1618, James was especially and violently aggressive in his attempts to force the Scotch people to accept episcopacy. These attempts were fully set forth by one David Calderwood, in his book entitled Perth Assembly. It was privately printed, and for a long time its origin was a mystery; but later it was surmised, from the similarity of the type to that of Brewster's confessed publications, that it had emanated from his press.

Of late years the British archives have been

searched for papers which might throw light upon the movements of the Separatists, before the emigration of the Scrooby church to New England, and with signal success. Among other papers have been discovered a series of letters written and received by Sir Dudley Carleton, who, at the time of which we write, was the British ambassador at The Hague. A letter dated July 17, 1619, addressed by Sir Dudley to Sir Robert Naunton, King James' secretary of state, is of peculiar interest in this connection. "I have seen," writes Sir Dudley, "within these two days a certain Scottish book called *Perth Assembly,* written with much scorn and reproach of the proceedings in that kingdom concerning the affairs of the church. It is without name, either of author or printer, but I am informed it is printed by a certain English Brownist of Leyden, as are most of the Puritan books sent over, of late days, into England. Which, being directly against an express *Placaat* of the States General, which was published in December last, I intend, when I have more particular knowledge of the printer to make complaint thereof, conceiving that His Majesty will not dislike that I should do so."

This information pointed directly at William Brewster and his printing plant, hidden in the attic of the house in Choir Alley in Leyden. But why such secrecy in Leyden, and what the meaning, in this free country of Holland, of this statement of Carleton's regarding a *Placaat,* or proclamation, of the States General? To explain this anomaly we must look to conditions in Spain, at that time. Now a weak nation of Europe, Spain was then powerful. All Europe had quailed before her, and to none save England, which had crushed and defeated the Invincible Armada, could Holland look for help in the threatened renewal of Spain's attack upon her. It behooved the States of Holland, therefore, to keep peace with England at all hazards; and when it was learned that attacks upon the king's majesty were printed in Holland and sent thence for circulation in England, it was felt that a certain degree of repression was necessary.

A later letter of Carleton, under date of July 22, 1619, shows that the ambassador had been diligent in following up the clew already found, and now he declares that this book, Perth Assembly, and another which had much disturbed the king, had both been printed by one William Brewster, a Brownist, "who hath been for some years an inhabitant and printer at Leyden, but is now removed from thence and gone back to dwell in London."

Now ensued a rigid hunt for William Brewster, but he was wary and was not to be found. When he was sought in London he was certainly in Leyden or Amsterdam; and when believed to be in a Dutch city, which city was ransacked in the search for him, he was surely in London. At one time his son was apprehended in London and his father's whereabouts sought from him. But his ignorance of his father's whereabouts was profound, and he himself could not be harmed, for, being closely watched by the king's spies, he was found to be regularly attending services on Sunday at the Established Church, and so was not amenable to discipline under the law.

The whereabouts of Brewster's types was finally learned, and the attic was raided by the authorities and the door nailed in two places and officially sealed with green wax. A bailiff, who was fond of his cups, was set to watch for Brewster and arrest him; but he made a mistake and arrested Brewer instead. But Brewer was a member of the University of Leyden and so entitled to certain privileges, among which was immunity from arrest. Later, however, he went voluntarily to London to be examined by the king in person; but having thus gone voluntarily, he was entitled to safe conduct and immunity from punishment and little was learned from him as to Brewster, and his doings. Meantime, as we know, Brewster was in England, quietly making arrangements for the emigration of the Leyden Church to New England. How he escaped arrest at this period of peculiar hazard no one knows. But his printing plant was confiscated, and after Brewster's removal to New England he made no attempt to renew it, feeling doubtless that to do so would bring the young and weak colony of Plymouth in too great hazard of the king's displeasure.

VI

THE VOYAGE OF THE MAYFLOWER

A S we have already seen, the Pilgrim colony remained in Holland for about twelve years, during which time they made an excellent impression upon the people among whom they dwelt. Their pastor, the Rev. John Robinson, received high honors from the University of Leyden. Mr. Brewster was held in great respect by the people of wealth and station, whose sons were sent to him for instruction in English. The rank and file of the congregation, many of whom were poor and all of whom labored for their daily bread, were honored by their Dutch neighbors for their strict integrity.

But, as time passed, the feeling grew stronger among them that they should seek another and a permanent place of abode, where they might preserve their own language and customs of life, while retaining their right to worship as conscience dictated. Bradford gives three reasons for this determination. The first of these was the hardness of their life in a foreign land. They followed occupations to which they were unaccustomed, and although they made thereby a comfortable livelihood, yet it was only by hard and continuous labor. Some friends from England joined themselves to the colony, but, finding it so difficult to gain a livelihood, they returned to England, though at great hazard of their lives and liberty. In addition to this, they began to realize that their children, by reason of hard labor, appeared to be growing old before their time. Then, too, they began to fear for the moral effect upon their children of the association with some of the young people about them. "By the manifold temptations of the place they were drawne away by evil examples into extravagant and dangerous courses." Not this alone, but the young people were beginning to intermarry with their Dutch neighbors, and they readily saw that it would, in the end, be impossible to maintain their English individuality, but that, in the course of time, they would inevitably become incorporated into the Dutch people. But above and beyond all else was a desire on the part of these people to find a place for a settlement by themselves, where they might worship as their own consciences dictated, apart from all political or ecclesiastical masters.

These reasons, added to the increasing activity of Sir Dudley Carleton, the English ambassador at The Hague, as noted in the preceding chapter, determined the Pilgrims to continue their pilgrimage and emigrate to America. This conclusion was not reached without careful consideration and earnest prayer for divine guidance. But when the decision was at length firmly reached, John Carver and Robert Cushman were appointed a special committee to proceed to London and make arrangements, if so they might be able, to remove the colony to America.

The place of the future colony was first considered. There were not a few of the company who favored a settlement in British Guiana, where the country was rich and fruitful and blessed with continual spring. Others favored a settlement in some portion of Virginia, for it was learned that there was already an English settlement in that region. Objections were found to both these suggestions: to the first by reason of the supposed unhealthfulness of a warm climate; to the other, that a proximity to an English colony already established might bring upon them persecution for the cause of religion, as in England itself. Finally it was decided to form a settlement by themselves, in some portion of the territory covered by the patent issued by the king to the London-Virginia Company, an organization devoting its energies to the promotion of colonization in America. The northernmost boundary of this grant was at about the mouth of the River Hudson, or the place now covered by the great city of New York. From this point northward to, or beyond, the coast of Maine, stretched the country covered by the patent granted to the London-Plymouth Company.

Through Sir Robert Naunton an effort was made to induce the king to grant to the prospective colony a patent, or charter, which should include in its terms a provision granting liberty of conscience. When the subject of a colony in America was broached to the king, he inquired by what means the colonists expected to gain a livelihood. "By fishing," he was told. " 'Tis an honest trade," said the king. "It was the apostles' own calling." But when the king was asked to grant a charter which should confer religious liberty, he demurred to putting such an agreement in writing, but intimated that they should not be disturbed if they conducted themselves properly. Indeed, Bradford says that "if there was no security in the promise intimated, there would be no great certainty in a further confirmation of the same; for if afterward there should be a purpose or desire to wrong them, though they had a seale as broad as a house floor it would not serve the turn, for there would be means enough found to recall or reverse it."

Carver and Cushman, in searching for means for financing the expedition, learned of the Company of Merchant Adventurers, which had been formed for the purpose of financially promoting colonies on the American coast, and with them, after much haggling, they succeeded in making a contract. Here began the troubles of the Plymouth Pilgrims, which were not soon discontinued. The agent of the Adventurers, one Thomas Weston, was a character whom, in the colloquialism of to-day, we should call a "shyster." He signed a contract with the agents of the emigrants, then forced them to modify it against their best interests. Finally he refused to pay the last installment of the money to be advanced for the voyage, and they were obliged to sell some of the provisions which they had purchased, in order to buy some necessary tools, fishing gear, and other outfittings. At last the company of Leyden colonists, who were to join the expedition, took their departure from the city and proceeded, probably by canal, to the port of Delfthaven, where they were to embark in a small vessel, of about sixty tons, called the Speedwell, which had been bought and fitted in Holland. This vessel was designed as a sort of tender or convoy to the larger ship, the Mayflower, which had been chartered in England for the voyage. The Speedwell was to remain in American waters, as the property of the colony, to be used in fishing and also in coastwise trading.

Not all the Leyden colony planned to go out in the first company. Indeed, the greater number remained behind, designing to join the colony after it should have become fairly established. Mr. Robinson, the pastor, was among those who remained behind, hoping to join the brethren in America at a later day, when the majority of the church should have gone over. As it resulted, he never saw Plymouth.

The story of the farewells of the Pilgrim company to those whom they left behind is full of pathos. Many of the Leyden people, who were to remain behind, accompanied the party to Delfthaven. The party reached the port near the close of the day and the night was spent, probably in the warehouses on the wharf, "with little sleepe by the most." The next morning the party went on board the vessel, "and their friends with them, where truly doleful was the sight of that sad and mournful parting." So sad it was that even some of the Dutch strangers who witnessed it could not themselves refrain from tears. But the parting must come and "the tide, which stays for no man, called them away." The pastor, John Robinson, at the last moment fell upon his knees on the deck and offered a fervent prayer for the success of the voyage. The sails were hoisted and "with a prosperous winde they came in short time to Southampton." The farewell discourse of Pastor Robinson has been alluded to in a previous chapter.

At Southampton they found the Mayflower lying ready for the voyage and with her a con-

ROBINSON'S PRAYER AT THE EMBARKATION

THE DEPARTURE FROM DELFTHAVEN, HOLLAND
From Griffi's Pilgrims in Their Three Homes, Houghton Mifflin Co., Boston

siderable company of Separatists from London, who had come thither to join the party. Twenty persons were allotted to go in the Speedwell and one hundred in the Mayflower. A governor and two or three assistants were chosen for each vessel, not to control the management of the vessels, but for the government of those on board. On the fifth day of August, with a favorable wind the little flotilla set sail upon the momentous voyage.

The two ships had proceeded about three hundred miles at sea, when the captain of the Speedwell signaled to the Mayflower that his vessel was leaking badly. The leak presently became so alarming that it was finally determind to put about for the port of Dartmouth. Here the vessel was thoroughly examined, but no especial leak was found, and after making a few repairs they again set sail. But after proceeding a considerable distance the leakage of the Speedwell again became alarming and once more the vessels put back, this time into the harbor of Plymouth. Here, after again vainly searching for the cause of the leakage, it was determined to abandon the Speedwell, and proceed alone with the Mayflower. Eighteen of the party were designated to remain behind, some on account of physical weakness, others by reason of their own desire to remain. The cargo was re-stowed, and at length, on September 6, after the loss of a full month of valuable time, the Mayflower, with one hundred and two emigrants on board, for the third time took its departure from England.

But for these delays the result of the voyage would unquestionably have been far different than it was. Had the voyage from Southampton been continuous, they would have escaped the autumn storms and would doubtless have reached their place of intended settlement, near the mouth of the Hudson River, while still the weather was agreeable. Had the Mayflower been of a rig better suited to buffeting the early autumn storms, she might have made port far sooner than she did. But during the one hundred and twenty-eight years that had passed since the little fleet of Columbus sailed out of the port of Palos, but small advance had been made in the construction of seagoing vessels. The Mayflower was so built and rigged that it was impossible to sail her in any direction except directly before the wind. When, therefore, she encountered head winds, as she did soon after leaving the port of Plym-

In the image, the banners read:

FOR THE LORD IS OUR DEFENCE

AND THE HOLY ONE OF ISRAEL IS OUR KING

THE PILGRIMS SIGHTING THE HIGHLANDS OF CAPE COD
From a Mural Painting by Henry O. Walker, State House, Boston

outh, she could do nothing but sail before them. Back and forth, up and down the Atlantic, she was driven, much of the time far out of her course. So fierce was the storm at times that the seamen were obliged to take in all sail and commit themselves to the fury of the wind under bare poles. Presently they were greatly alarmed at the discovery that, so badly was the vessel's hull wrenched by the force of the sea and the wind, a great main beam, which supported the upper works of the ship, was beginning to buckle. Fortunately, one of the passengers had brought with him a powerful jackscrew, and with the aid of this instrument the beam was forced back into place and safely secured, so that this danger passed.

For two months and five days the voyage continued, to the great weariness of the Pilgrim voyagers both in body and spirit. One death occurred during the voyage, that of a young man named William Button; and a son was born to the wife of Stephen Hopkins, to whom was given the name of Oceanus. On the tenth day of November, 1620, they sighted land, but instead of the coast which they sought, they soon found that the land in sight was the bold highland of Cape Cod, on which to-day stands the great flashing coast light known to mariners as Highland Light.

Disappointed, they put about and turned the vessel's prow southward; but when they had proceeded in this direction for some hours they "fell amongst deangerous shoulds and roring breakers, and they were so farr intangled therwith, as they conceived themselves in great danger." Undoubtedly they were in dangerous proximity to the shoals of Pollock Rip and the low, sandy spit of Monomoy. The fear of shipwreck, which assailed them, was by no means idle, and prudently they again put about and bore up for the harbor of Cape Cod. Night was approaching and without a chart it was not at all easy for the navigators of the ship to find their way into the harbor. The cape, at its extremity, sweeps about, in shape like a mighty sickle, inclosing the harbor save at the entrance. "The bay is so round and circling," wrote Winslow, "that, before we could come to anchor, we went round all the points of the compass."

The harbor in which they first dropped anchor was that now known as that of Provincetown. The Mayflower reached this port on Saturday, the eleventh day of November,

SIGNING OF THE COMPACT IN THE CABIN OF THE MAYFLOWER

LANDING PLACE OF PILGRIMS, LONG POINT

1620. Anchor was dropped, beyond doubt in the deep water just inside of Long Point, for Winslow records that "they found it to be a small neck of land. On this side where we lay is the bay and on the further side the sea," a description exactly fitting the locality suggested. "Being thus arrived in a good harbor and brought safe to land," says Bradford, "they fell upon their knees and blessed the God of heaven, who had brought them over the vast and furious ocean and delivered them from all the periles and miseries thereof, againe to set their feete on the firme and stable earth, their proper elemente."

But one of the most important acts known to history has been omitted in the narrative. The patent granted to the prospective colony was for a settlement within the territory granted by the crown to the London-Virginia Company. The place where they had determined to land was within the territory of the Plymouth-Virginia Company. The Pilgrims had, therefore, no warrant for making a settlement here, and of this fact all on board were well aware. Some there were among the party who were with the company, but not of them. Some of these were men servants; some were the common sailors, who must perforce remain among them for some months to come. Whisperings were overheard among some of these. "These people," said they, "have no charter for a settlement at Cape Cod, and without a charter they have no authority over us. We will, therefore, when we come ashore use our own liberty."

Brewster and Carver, Bradford and Winslow, and Standish, mighty with the sword, were equal to this emergency. Upon the lid of Standish's chest—which one may see, any day, in Pilgrim Hall, at Plymouth—they drew up and signed that immortal Compact of government, by which this company "solemnly and mutually in the presence of God and of one another," did "covenant and combine" themselves "together into a civill body politick." Here was the germ root of our great republic, the first charter of a government for the people and by the people known to human history. This historic occurrence is the subject of one of the great paintings in the rotunda of the Capitol at Washington. It is also commemorated, as a notable occurrence in English history, in a splendid mural painting in the Houses of Parliament in London.

VII

THE PILGRIMS AT CAPE COD

NO period of time in the Pilgrim story is more memorable than the five or six weeks passed at Cape Cod, immediately after the landing upon the American shore and prior to the formation of the settlement at Plymouth. The landing, as we already know, was upon the "small neck of land," now known as Long Point. This neck of land, now devoid of growth, save a sparse covering of beach grass, was at that time covered with a thick wood, in which oaks, pines, sassafras, juniper, birch, and holly were intermingled. This thick growth of wood did not extend to the very extremity of the point, but came to an abrupt end a mile or so to the west, a circumstance which gave the name of Wood End to this vicinity, a name which still survives in those of a government lighthouse and coast guard station. It was doubtless upon the narrowest, and unwooded, part of the point where the Pilgrims made their landing, and where they probably built some temporary shelters of boughs.

As soon as the landing was made, on Saturday, the 11th of November, a party of fifteen or sixteen men was hastily made up, for a superficial examination of their position. The party spent the remainder of the day in observations, returning at nightfall. It is probable that the party crossed the harbor in the ship's longboat, making a landing upon the northern shore, where is now the town of Provincetown, for the record says that they returned at night, their boat filled with juniper, which smelled very sweet and strong and of which they made their fires during their stay at the Cape. They saw no natives nor habitations in this brief journey of a November afternoon, and returned before the hour at which their Sabbath began. The next day, being Sunday, was doubtless passed in rest and worship, but at an early hour on Monday, November 13, the women of the party clamored to be set on shore, that they might wash the clothing of the company, "as they had great need." And thus was established the Monday wash day, which has persisted to the present time.

They had brought from England a shallop, or small sailing vessel, having a single mast and a square sail, stretched between two immovable yards. This shallop they had stowed between decks, on board the Mayflower, and to do this they had been obliged to cut her down. During the voyage she had become somewhat strained and her seams opened by the weight of the passengers, who were in the habit of lying in her, so that extensive repairs must be made before she could be used in exploring the coast. The ship carpenter, after working a day or two, became convinced that he had no quick and easy task before him, and the party, impatient to be moving, resolved to make an exploring expedition by land, in search of a place of settlement. It may be asked why they did not remain on the shores of this beautiful harbor and make their settlement there. Strangely enough, although at the present day there are many acres of thickly tangled woods in Provincetown, there is no actual arable land. The scores of garden plots, where vegetables and flowers grow luxuriantly to-day, have all been artificially formed, by soil brought thither in vessels from time to time and spread over the yellow sand.

The Pilgrims, in their brief Saturday afternoon journey on land, perceived that vegetables and grain for their sustenance would not readily grow here and they were quickly convinced that they must make perhaps an extended exploration, to discover that much needed combination, a good harbor and a productive soil. Indeed, it proved that three journeys of discovery were necessary before a place suitable for settlement was found.

It was the morning of Wednesday, November 15, that they set out upon the first of these journeys of discovery. The party was well organized and armed. It comprised sixteen men, under the leadership of Captain Myles Standish. The sword that hung at his side may be seen to-day, sacredly preserved in a glass case, in Pilgrim Hall at Plymouth. A council of advisers comprised William Bradford, Stephen Hopkins, and Edward Tilley. The party was set on shore, probably on the point where they had made their landing four days before, and set out boldly in single file. They had not gone far when they espied a small party of men, with a dog, approaching them. These proved to be Indians, the first whom the Pilgrims had seen. The natives fled before the approach of the white men, ran up a slope and disappeared in the woods. The Pilgrims followed the foottracks of the Indians for several miles, but failed to overtake them.

The Pilgrim party during the first day of their march must have compassed the entire northerly side of the great circling harbor. When night came upon them they made a camp in the open. They had no tents nor other shelter, and could do nothing more for their own comfort than to build a fire and perhaps cut a few boughs of trees to form their beds upon the cold ground, and a shelter from the wind. It must be remembered that this was mid November, and although this season is sometimes wonderfully mild and genial, who of us would care to make a three days' journey on foot over the bleak slopes and hollows of far Cape Cod, and sleep at night without covering upon the half-frozen, sodden earth? Yet this was what our Pilgrim Fathers were forced to do. And the second night proved of greater discomfort than the first, for the rain fell in torrents, and they had no shelter from the fury of the storm save a hastily made screen of logs, stakes, and boughs.

The first journey brought some interesting

experiences. The first day brought with it weariness and thirst, but in the forenoon of the second day, in a deep valley in the limits of the present town of Truro, they came upon a beautiful spring of sweet water, and the records say, "We sat us down and drank our first New England water, with as much delight as ever we drank drink in all our lives." This spring still bubbles brightly and is often visited by travelers on Cape Cod. A few miles beyond, they found the stubble of Indian corn —for here the land was higher and somewhat more fertile than at the point—and some hickory trees with nuts, and, in the hollows, fields of red cranberries, which these English travelers mistook for strawberries. Farther on, upon a hillslope they came upon a mound, into which they dug, and there found a great basket with three or four bushels of Indian corn, some of which they took with them. Some months later, as we shall learn, they encountered the owners of this corn and recompensed them for it, thereby gaining their friendship. But for this corn, which served them as seed the coming spring, the colonists of Plymouth must inevitably have perished. The hillslope they called Corn Hill, and Corn Hill it is to-day, a small granite monument marking the place of the discovery of the corn.

This discovery was followed by the stormy night already described, which must have brought with it great discomfort. But the next morning they met with a humorous experience; for in passing through the woods they came to a place where a strong sapling was bent down to the ground, with a rope of braided bark circled about and acorns scattered around. It was an Indian deer-trap, as the party soon learned, for the dignified William Bradford, in his curiosity, ventured too near the contrivance and was presently caught by the leg, in the springing of the trap, and so, without ceremony, swung into the air. Continuing their march, they saw deer and game birds, but do not seem to have shot any, for the birds were described as very wild. And so they returned to the shore and saw the Mayflower at anchor far across the harbor, some six or eight miles away. Those on board heard their signal guns and came across in the longboat, and so ended the first journey of discovery.

The exposure which they suffered in this journey bore its fruit, for several were made ill, and during the stay of the Pilgrims at the harbor of Cape Cod, six of their company died. It was not difficult to reach the shore of the point, near which the Mayflower lay, but save at high tide it was difficult—even as it is to-day—to reach the shore upon the opposite side of the harbor, by reason of the shallow water, especially in the western part. They were forced often to wade knee-deep in chilling water to reach this portion of the shore, and here grew the heaviest timber, which was necessary for the rebuilding of the shallop, and for the construction of a second, which was a necessity.

On Monday, the 27th of November, the repairs upon the shallop being so nearly complete that it was possible to use her, they set out upon the second journey of discovery. Twenty-four men of the Pilgrim company, besides ten members of the ship's crew, composed this second party. Difficulties at once beset them, for the weather was rough and the winds contrary. Some in the shallop and some in the longboat, they set out, but head winds forced them to row, and the day was far spent and the men nearly exhausted when they at length grounded in shallow water and were obliged to wade struggling to land. They had scarcely landed on shore when they were struck by a New England blizzard of blinding snow and piercing wind from the northeast, just such a blizzard as that which swept over this place on another 27th day of November, in 1898, in which the steamer Portland foundered, while all on board perished. "Some of our people that are dead," says the chronicle, "took the original of their death here." A dreadful night must this have been, in which the party bivouacked in the open, sleeping upon the snow-covered ground amid the storm and in the piercing cold.

But the next day they made some geographical discoveries—a little harbor, a small inlet or river, now called Pamet River; but they made their way over slopes, knee-deep in snow, and through hollows where lay still deeper drifts. They found nothing until, just at night, they came upon a little clump of pine trees, where they made their bivouac for the night. Three fat wild geese and a half dozen ducks had been shot, and these were roasted before the fire and formed their supper. The next day they stumbled again upon the hillside where they had found the corn and found about ten bushels more, which they regarded as "God's good Providence." Another comfortless night followed. Some of the party had fallen ill and could go no farther. These were sent back to the ship in the shallop, and those who were able pushed on. And now they began to come upon signs of human habitation, Indian wigwams and presently an Indian graveyard; but no natives were encountered. Without further important adventures the company, near nightfall, returned to the ship, and so ended the second journey, with few results.

A council was now held in the cabin to decide upon their future movements. Some urged that a settlement be made at Corn Hill. Here was a good harbor for boats; good corn ground not far away; an excellent place for fishing; and the place was easily defensible. To search farther, too, in this weather was hazardous. Others urged a removal to Angoum (now Ipswich), where, they had heard, was a good harbor and fertile land. Coppin, the ship's pilot, told of a good harbor about three leagues to the westward (Plymouth harbor), and it was at length determined to go upon a third journey of discovery, a journey which was productive of great results. The start was made on the 6th of December, the cold being intense. To follow the party through all the details of their adventures would occupy too great space. Their hardships and sufferings were terrible. Their bivouacs were as before on the cold and sodden earth without shelter. On the second day out they reached the part of the Cape where now is the town of Eastham. At midnight of the previous night they had been awakened by hideous cries, which came from the woods beyond them. The sentinel cried, "Arm! Arm!" and all seized their weapons, expecting an attack. But the sounds died away and nothing more was heard during the night. But soon after daylight, while some of the party were at the camp and others near the shallop by the shore, the shouts and cries were suddenly renewed. "Their note," says the narrative, "was after this manner: 'Woath! woach! ha! ha! hach! woach!'"

All ran to arms and a moment later a shower of arrows fell about them, while the hideous shouting was redoubled. Several shots were fired at the attacking party and especially at one "lusty man and no whit less valiant," who seemed to be the leader and who was partially hidden behind a tree. Presently a bullet struck the tree close by his head and with a strange cry he and his companions fled and the party of explorers was no more disturbed. A number of the arrows were gathered where they had fallen and being made into a bundle were sent to England, as souvenirs of the encounter.

The excitement of the attack being over, the Pilgrims continued their journey. Embarking in the shallop, which had followed the party in their movements upon land, they made the remainder of the journey by water. Snow began to fall, succeeded by a cold rain and heavy wind. The rudder was broken by the rough sea. Darkness overtook them—the storm increased in severity. Land appeared through the blackness of the night. The shallop was beached, and, struggling through the waves, they reached the shore. The morning came, and the party, drenched and shivering, found themselves upon a small island, now called Clarke's Island. Here they remained through the day, the storm being too severe for further explorations. This was Saturday, the 9th of December. The next day the storm had cleared, but it was the Sabbath day, and "on the Sabbath Day we rested."

The next morning, Monday, December 21,

LONG POINT, PROVINCETOWN

THE MAYFLOWER AT ANCHOR AT PLYMOUTH
From a painting by W. F. Halsall

N. S., they sounded the harbor and found it of good depth for shipping. Approaching the mainland near the mouth of a brook, they came to a sandy beach beneath a low cliff, where, at the water's edge lay a great bowlder, dropped ages ago by some migratory arctic glacier. Stepping upon it and thence to the beach constituted the historic "Landing of the Pilgrims." It was a simple act but one fraught with the mightiest consequences, for that one solitary bowlder thus became consecrated as *Plymouth Rock,* "the corner stone of a nation."

This exploring party, which had left the Mayflower in Cape Cod harbor and had coasted around the bay, landed at Plymouth and fixed upon it as the place of their permanent settlement, was made up, as Bradford says, of "ten of their principal men." Mourt's Relation is more specific, for it gives the names as follows:

Captain Myles Standish, Governor John Carver, William Bradford, Edward Winslow, John Tilley, Edward Tilley, John Howland, all of the Leyden company; Richard Warren, Stephen Hopkins, and Edward Dotey, of London, who were of the party who joined the Pilgrim company at Southampton. In addition to these two of the Pilgrim seamen, John

Allerton and Thomas English, were of the party. To manage the shallop Captain Jones of the Mayflower sent with them his two mates, Clarke and Coppin, the master gunner and three common seamen. Thus the shallop contained eighteen men, twelve of the Pilgrim company and six of the Mayflower's men.

They marched into the land and "found divers cornfields and little running brooks, a place very good for situation." At last they had found a place suitable for settlement and they returned to Cape Cod with the joyful news. It was both a sad and a joyous returning, for during the absence of the expedition Dorothy May, the sweet, young wife of William Bradford, by some mischance had fallen overboard from the Mayflower and had lost her life by drowning. But the sadness was mingled with joy, for during their absence Susanna White, the wife of William White, had become the mother of a fine boy, whom she named Peregrine—the first white child born in New England.

On the 15th day of December (December 25, N. S.), the Mayflower, after a stay at Cape Cod of upward of a month, weighed anchor and sailed away to Plymouth harbor.

VIII

THE PILGRIMS AT PLYMOUTH

WHEN the Mayflower dropped her anchor in the harbor of Plymouth, the Pilgrims doubtless felt that their tribulations were well-nigh past. They had suffered troublous days during the preparations for the voyage at the hands of the Merchant Adventurers, and had at last been obliged to sail with a short supply of provisions. They were delayed a full month by the unseaworthiness of the Speedwell, and were finally forced to leave her behind, with a portion of the party. They were buffeted by storms, driven far from the course, and finally, after a voyage of upwards of two months, had been obliged to land more than one hundred miles north of their intended destination. For nearly six weeks they had suffered terrible hardships in their search for a place of settlement. At last, storm-tossed and distressed almost to the extremity, they had found a harbor and a place suitable for the founding of their projected colony, and their ship, sheltered from the most powerful of the blasts of a New England winter, swung peacefully at anchor. Well may they have felt that their tribulations were well-nigh over. Indeed, they had hardly begun. Here was, it is true, an excellent harbor; here were apparently fertile fields ready, when springtime should come, for the plowing and sowing. Their seed corn had come, as it seemed to them, in as miraculous a way as had come the manna to the children of Israel in the wilderness. They had formed a Compact of government, and a little later John Carver was elected the first governor of the colony.

But they were in the midst of a northern winter and they were poorly prepared to meet its rigors. They had anticipated an arrival at a more southerly point and in the sunny glow of the early autumn days. In both anticipations they had been disappointed. They had, to be sure, found a place of settlement, but materials for building dwellings formed no part of their cargo. Axes they had, to be sure, but few other tools, and their building materials must be wrested from the virgin forest. Their occupations in Holland had given them little practice in swinging the ax, felling trees, in hewing out logs and planks, in hauling them to place and building up the walls of the log huts which must form their habitations. They had no horses nor oxen to aid them in hauling the logs, and probably but little tackle with which to raise them to place. All must be done by sheer human force, and this labor in the freezing cold must have been exhausting in the extreme.

The labor was too severe and the suffering from the cold too great for some of the less rugged, and these soon began to succumb. Not only this, but the two months of close confinement on shipboard, during the voyage, added to the hardships at Cape Cod, had developed in many the seeds of scurvy. All possible haste was made in erecting some houses for shelter on shore, so that the company, as soon as possible, might be removed from the confining quarters of the ship. But at the best it was slow work and long before a sufficient number of humble shelters had been built, many of the workers were prostrated by sickness. The terrible plague which soon swept over the company was, doubtless, scurvy, mingled with pneumonia. Of the party,

Fuller alone was possessed of any medical
knowledge, and the prostration of so great a
number of the colonists overwhelmed him with
labor. Not only those on shore were smitten,
but those as well who still kept their quarters
in the ship. Labor was abandoned, and those
who were spared from an attack of the illness
were made ill themselves by caring for the sick.

Bradford, in pathos deep, records the story
of that first dreadful winter in the Plymouth
Colony. "But that which was most sadd and
lamentable," he writes, "was that in two or
three months' time half of their company dyed,
especially in January and February, being the
depth of winter and wanting houses and other
comforts, being infected with the scurvie and
other diseases, which this long voyage and their
inacomodate condition had brought upon
them; so as there dyed sometimes two or three
of a day in the aforesaid time, that, of one
hundred and odd persons, scarce fifty remained. And of these in the time of most distress there was but six or seven sound persons
who, to their great comendations be it spoken,
spared no pains, night or day, but with abundance of toyle and hazard of their owne health,
fetched them wood, made their fires, drest them

meat, made their beds, washed their loathsome cloaths, cloathed and uncloathed them, in a word did all the homely and necessarie offices for them and all this willingly and cheerfully, without any grudging in the least, shewing herein their true love unto their friends and brethren."

The most pathetic part of this shocking tragedy was the great mortality among the mothers of families. Of sixteen such women, but four remained alive when spring opened and the sickness in the colony began to abate. Of twenty-five fathers of families—some of whom had left their wives in Holland—thirteen succumbed to the sickness. So many were the dead that those who remained alive could scarcely bury them; and when at last the spring opened, the graves were leveled with the ground and the field sown with grain, lest the Indians, who had terrorized the settlement by much prowling about, should learn of the weakness of the colony by counting the graves of the dead.

But at last the long, cruel winter passed away, the springtime came, and with its coming the epidemic of illness began to abate. The remaining dwellings were completed and all were able to leave the ship and begin their lives in their new home. The summer came on, and with it the households, broken by death, were in a measure again erected. There were widows and children to be cared for and, in the exigencies of the situation, this could best be done through marriages with husbands bereft of wives. To our minds it is not a little startling to read that, but a few short weeks after the cessation of the mortality in the colony, Edward Winslow—afterward the governor—whose wife had been a victim of the great sickness, was married to Susanna, the widow of William White and mother of the infant Peregrine. There were not a few of these occurrences, and there were some romances as well among the young people of the colony. Longfellow, in immortal verse, has celebrated the marriage of John Alden to Priscilla Mullins, left doubly an orphan in the great sickness. Mary Chilton, an orphan likewise, was married to John, the brother of Edward Winslow. Those who pass along the walk by the old burying-ground on Tremont Street, in Boston, may see, through the iron palings, her grave, where she lies almost beneath the shadow of King's Chapel. It was Mary Chilton,

PLYMOUTH ROCK

so says the tradition, who first of the company stepped foot upon Plymouth Rock.

And so, when the dark cloud of sickness and death at last passed over, the little colony, bereft of half its number, took up the thread of the broken lives. A street was laid out running back from the sea to the foot of the hill in the rear of the tiny settlement. Leyden Street it was called by the people of later days in memory of the city "of sweet situation," where the Pilgrims passed so many very happy days, and Leyden Street it is to-day. Meersteads and garden plots were laid out and allotted to the several families, and when the time for planting came these plots were planted in corn.

It should be here noted that the Pilgrim company, from the time of breaking up their homes in Holland, like those of the primitive church, "had all things in common." Each family sold all that it had and put the proceeds of the sale into a common fund, and there was no Ananias nor Sapphira among them.

It was with the funds so raised that the Speedwell was purchased for the use of the colony. It was the agreement with the Merchant Adventurers that the labor of all the colonists should belong to the common stock, and that the advances made by the Adventurers for financing the expedition should be made good by shipments of salted fish and other commodities which the country yielded. At the outset, then, the division of lands into homestead lots was made only for present use and not for inheritance. Indeed, every bushel of corn which was raised during the first few years was turned into a common granary and issued to the colonists in equal portions as was needed. The completion of the log houses for dwellings was no small task, and it was not until the spring was far advanced that this labor was completed.

While they were thus occupied and before the sickness among the people had fully abated, one day the settlers were surprised and startled at the appearance of an Indian in the street of the village. Many times during the winter and spring they had been alarmed at the sight of small bands of Indians prowling about in woods, and on one occasion some tools which had been left in a small clearing, while the workmen were at dinner, had been stolen. The colonists were still more surprised when they were accosted by this visiting Indian in fairly good English, who bade them "Welcome." This visitor was Samoset, a member of a tribe to the northward. From him they learned that there was an English fishing station on the coast of Maine, which was in frequent communication with the home country. By mingling with these English fishermen Samoset had acquired some knowledge of their language. Through Samoset the settlers learned of another Indian, named Squanto, or Tisquantum, who was still better versed in English than himself. Squanto afterward came and for some years made his home with the Plymouth people. His name is preserved in the name of the peninsula of Squantum, which projects into Boston Bay, just south of the River Neponset.

Squanto proved to be a friend of the greatest value to the people of Plymouth. He had, it appeared, some years before been kidnapped by the crew of an English vessel and with several other natives taken away to be sold as a slave to the Spaniards. It is not known how Squanto escaped and made his way to London, but that he did so is certain and that he lived in that city several years, acquiring a very good knowledge of the English language. He at length made his way back to his native country to find that he was nearly the sole survivor of his tribe, which had inhabited the region in which the settlement of Plymouth had been made. A year or two before the Mayflower dropped anchor here, a strange plague, the nature of which has never been determined, had swept over this region, slaying the natives by hundreds, and with such awful swiftness that many of the dead lay unburied in their crumbling wigwams.

The place where Plymouth had been settled was known to the Indians as Patuxet. Here Squanto had been born and reared, and when he returned from England and discovered what a calamity had befallen his people, the impulse came to him to remain in his old home with these new found friends. Squanto was, so Governor Bradford records, "their interpreter and was a special instrument sent by God for their good beyond their expectation." He at once made himself at home at Plymouth. At the first glance he saw that the colony was short of provisions and he "went at noon to fish for eels. At night he came home with as many as he could well lift in one hand, which our people were glad of. They were fat and sweet. He trod them out with his feete and so caught them with his hands, without any other instrument." He pointed out to them the best fields for raising corn and told them that the time for planting was when the young leaves upon the oak trees were of the size of a mouse's ear. He taught them how to plant corn, with a fish in each hill for fertilizing, for "except they gott fish and set with it, in these old grounds it would come to nothing." He told them that in the middle of April great quantities of herring would come up the brook and he taught them how to build weirs, or traps, to catch them. Thus he supplied them both with food and with fertilizing material for their crops.

It was about this time that the captain and crew of the Mayflower began to make preparations for the return voyage. It had been impossible for her to return earlier, for several reasons. Perhaps the reason which chiefly influenced the captain and crew was the tempestuous weather which prevailed throughout the winter. In addition to this, the ship was necessary to the colonists for a place of shelter while the houses were in the process of building. The epidemic of illness which soon prevailed made it absolutely impossible for the ship to sail, for many of the crew were themselves prostrated. The Merchant Adventurers expected a return cargo and the hope of being able to meet this expectation, in some degree at least, was probably an additional reason for the delay. And so the spring was well advanced when the Mayflower hoisted her sails and sailed away toward the rising sun.

Artists have depicted the little handful of quaintly dressed Pilgrims grouped upon the shore and sorrowfully watching the white sails as they gradually grew less and finally dipped down beneath the horizon and disappeared. It was the sole link which connected the Pilgrim band with their old home. What sufferings and distresses had this faithful band not passed through since they left their homes in Scrooby and went out into the world in search of a place where they might worship undisturbed by priest or magistrate. But sufferings extreme had not shaken the faith of this noble company. The Mayflower sailed away, but did she carry with her any faint-hearted ones, ready to abandon the struggle?

Nay! One text was burned into their hearts, it was as frontlets between their eyes: "No man, having put his hand to the plough,

THE RETURN OF THE MAYFLOWER

THE COMING OF THE FORTUNE—See page 133

and looking back, is fit for the kingdom of God."

"O strong hearts and true! not one went back in the Mayflower!

No, not one looked back, who had set his hand to this ploughing!

Long in silence they watched the receding sail of the vessel,

Much endeared to them all, as something living and human;

Then as if filled with the Spirit, and wrapt in a vision prophetic,

Baring his hoary head the excellent elder of Plymouth

Said: 'Let us pray!' and they prayed and thanked the Lord and took courage."

IX

PLYMOUTH'S TREATY WITH MASSASOIT

IMPORTANT to the colonists as was the coming to them of Squanto, the visit of Samoset bore still richer fruit. Samoset was in reality the herald of an embassy which was on its way from Massasoit, the great sachem of the Wampanoags. Indeed, Massasoit himself led the party of warrior-visitors, a fact which greatly enhanced the importance of the embassy. The tribe of Wampanoags had their seat on the east shore of Narragansett Bay; the fierce tribe of the Narragansetts, led by Canonicus, occupied the region on the west shore. Through Squanto, no doubt, the colonists learned the importance of the great and powerful tribe of the Wampanoags, led by Massasoit, who was, beyond doubt, the most powerful and influential chief in all the region, from Narragansett Bay to the extremity of Cape Cod. The tribe to which Squanto had belonged, and which formerly inhabited the region in which the Pilgrims had settled, had, as we already know, been nearly obliterated by a deadly plague. There was a small tribe, called the Pocassets, in the region east of the Wampanoags and west of the Pilgrim settlement; another at Manomet, south of Plymouth, led by the sachem Canacum; still another small tribe on the Cape, near the present town of Barnstable, led by the young sachem Iyanough; and the further part of the Cape was inhabited by the tribe of Nausets. This last-named tribe it was which attacked the Pilgrim exploring party on their third journey of discovery. Besides these, there was still another tribe on the island of Capawack, now known as Martha's Vineyard. North of Plymouth, in the region of Boston Bay, was the remnant of a tribe led by a bad Indian, called Wituwamat. None of these tribes was actually tributary to the Wampanoags, but all were much smaller and weaker than they and the influence of Massasoit was great among them.

The Pilgrims well understood that, could they form friendly relations with Massasoit, they would be upon good terms also with all the Indians of the entire region. It was therefore with the greatest interest that they learned from Samoset that Massasoit, with a party of followers, was approaching the settlement upon a friendly mission. The colony had now assumed the appearance of a small village. A large, square common house, built of logs, stood upon the hill back of the town. This was used as a place of worship, as a fort, and also as a place for the holding of town meetings, for the New England town meeting was inaugurated in Plymouth at an early period of the settlement. On the one street of the village there were seven dwelling houses, besides one or two buildings for the storage of provisions and supplies.

It was in March, following the settlement of Plymouth in December, 1620, that Samoset stalked into the village. In the seventeenth century, it must be remembered, the calendar year began on March 25, and not on January 1, as at present, so that the visit of Samoset must be dated in March, 1620. He was attired in the Indian manner, wearing but little clothing. He bore a bow and two arrows, one of which was without a head. After announcing himself and paying a brief visit, he went away, promising to return the next day.

TREATY WITH MASSASOIT

In this short visit the colonists learned that he was the sachem of a tribe at Monhegan, on the Maine coast, and that he had acquired his knowledge of the English language through the crews of the fishing vessels which frequented that place. He was visiting among the Wampanoags and had acted as a herald and interpreter for Massasoit, at that sachem's request, because of his knowledge of the white man's tongue.

The next day he returned with a little party of five or six braves, attired like himself. They left their weapons some distance from the village and brought with them the tools which had been stolen during the winter. The visitors were hospitably entertained, but since it was the Sabbath, the Plymouth people declined to trade with the Indians. They presently went away, leaving a number of beaver skins which they desired to barter for the white men's goods. A few days later Samoset and his friends returned again, now announcing the coming of Massasoit and a party of sixty warriors. An hour later, this formidable body of Indians appeared on a hilltop, a short distance south of the village, making friendly signs to the colonists. The first appearance of

Squanto in Plymouth was with this party of
Wampanoags. Without hesitation he came
into the village and asked that a messenger be
sent to meet Massasoit. Edward Winslow
volunteered for this seemingly hazardous service and the colonists, not without anxiety,
watched him go down the slope, cross the brook
at the ford, and ascend the slope on the opposite side, disappearing from the sight of his
friends in the company of savages.

The interview of Winslow with Massasoit
was mutually pleasing, and presently, leaving
Winslow as a hostage, the sachem took twenty
of his braves and started for the village.
Standish and Allerton, of the Pilgrim company, with six musketeers, met the chief at the
ford of the brook, received him with military
honors, and escorted him into the settlement.
In the common house the sachem was received
by Governor Carver, with such pomp as could
be mustered, and he and his escort were entertained with food and drink. The interview
ended in the conclusion of a treaty of peace.
In recording these events, twenty-four years
afterward, Governor Bradford said that this
peace had never been broken. Indeed, this
pact, the first ever made between white men

HEROIC STATUE OF MASSASOIT
C. E. Dallin, Sculptor

and Indians, was never broken. The savage, Massasoit, regarded his written promise as something far more important than a mere "scrap of paper."

The obligation into which Massasoit entered with Governor Carver was very simple and comprised six ties. Massassoit agreed that neither he nor any of his should in any way injure the colonists; if any subject of Massasoit should injure one of them, he would send him to Plymouth for punishment. It was mutually agreed that if anything should be taken from either party it should be restored, and if any should make war upon either party, the other would be confederate with the attacked. Massasoit agreed to certify the existence of this treaty to the neighboring tribes. In any visit made by the Indians to their white neighbors, their bows and arrows should be left behind. How unfortunate that the treaty guaranteeing the integrity of Belgium should not have been signed by a Massasoit in place of a William of Prussia!

This treaty with Massasoit proved to be of the greatest value to the Plymouth colony. In the entire history of the colony the settlement was never attacked by Indians. A few years after this, it is true, a wide-spread conspiracy, directed against all white settlers on the coast, was formed among the lesser tribes above named; but Massasoit, becoming aware of it, sent information to Plymouth, enabling the colonists effectually to forestall and prevent an attack. This important episode in Old Colony history will be considered more at length in a later chapter.

It was perhaps two weeks after the conclusion of the treaty with Massasoit that the Mayflower sailed upon her return voyage. Scarcely had the ship disappeared from sight when the colonists, under the direction of Squanto, began vigorous work in their fields. All who were able to work joined in the labor of preparing the ground for their crops and planting their corn. Even Governor Carver, although advanced in life, went into the field with the others and worked steadily. It was now the middle of April and, the winter being now fully past, the sun poured its rays down upon the field with great power. Governor Carver, unused to a New England winter, was unaware also of the strength and power of the New England spring sunshine. Working with ardor, he no doubt perspired freely and bared his head to the sun. He soon began to feel ill and presently returned to his log house, complaining of intense pains in his head. A little later he fell into a torpor from which he never rallied, and a few days later he passed away, to the great distress of the entire colony. No doubt his death was caused by sunstroke.

It was the Pilgrim custom to lay away their dead from sight with great simplicity. No prayer was uttered, lest it might be thought by some that prayers for the dead were a part of their religious belief. But so great was the reverence in which Governor Carver was held by all, "he was buried in the best manner they could." The military form was used and a volley of shots was fired over his grave by those who bore arms. The wife of the governor, "being a weak woman, dyed within five or six weeks after him," and thus was obliterated another of the Pilgrim households. We know really but little of Governor Carver. He was not one of the original party of the Pilgrims who fled from Scrooby, but was one of those who joined themselves to the Leyden colonists after their settlement in that place. He is first mentioned by Bradford as a deacon of the church and a coagent with Robert Cushman for making the arrangements for the voyage of the Mayflower. He appears to have been a man of much discretion and of great value to the colonists as a counselor. His death, says Bradford, "was much lamented and caused great heaviness amongst them."

Not long after the death of Governor Carver, William Bradford was chosen to be the chief magistrate of the colony in his stead. This occurred in April, 1621. By successive annual elections Bradford held this important office until 1633, when, protesting against so great a continued honor, he was succeeded by Edward Winslow. The next year Thomas Prence was elected governor, but in 1635 and again in 1637 Bradford was again placed in the governor's chair, which each time he filled for a year. In 1639 he was again elected governor and held the office for five years, being again succeeded by Edward Winslow. In 1645 he was still again returned to office and held the position of chief magistrate for twelve years more. In 1682 his eldest son, also named William Bradford, was elected deputy governor, holding that position for four years. Once more, in 1689, he was returned to the same office, which he held for a further term of three years. In all, therefore, William Bradford served the colony of Plymouth as its governor for thirty-one years and his son served as deputy governor for seven years. Unfortunately, no known portrait of Governor Bradford exists. His first wife, Dorothy, as we know already, lost her life by drowning while her husband was absent on the third journey of discovery. Two or three years later a friend of his early years, Alice Carpenter, now the Widow Southworth, came over from Leyden and became his wife. Their descendants in our country are numerous.

X

EARLY DAYS IN PLYMOUTH

THE obsequies of Governor Carver being over, William Bradford being elected governor in his stead, and the corn being all planted, it was determined to cement the friendship with Massasoit by sending an embassy to visit him. Edward Winslow and Stephen Hopkins were appointed to perform that honorable and hazardous office. They knew nothing of the country westward from Plymouth, but they had, in their brief intercourse with Massasoit and his followers, divined enough of the Indian character to understand that unhesitating boldness would always command their respect. With Squanto as a guide, therefore, the two envoys set out on foot for the home of Massasoit, on the east bank of Narragansett Bay. The place was fully forty miles distant from Plymouth. There was then not a horse nor other beast of burden in this portion of the American continent. Railway trains and automobiles had of course not been dreamed of; they had absolutely no means of conveyance. On foot, therefore, they set out.

The exact date of the setting out of this expedition is in doubt. Winslow, who wrote a narrative of his experiences, which narrative has been preserved, fixed the date as June 10, 1621. But as this date fell on Sunday, and since it is extremely improbable that they would have set out on the Lord's Day, it is believed that Winslow was mistaken in his date. Bradford says that the expedition set out on Monday, July 2. The first stage of the journey was as far as Namasket, now Middleboro, a distance of about fifteen miles. Here was an Indian village, inhabited by people of the tribe of Wampanoags, under the sway of Massasoit.

Many of the details of the journey, as recorded by Winslow, are of great interest. By the way, they fell in with many Indians, some of whom had previously visited Plymouth, asking for food. While the Pilgrims were glad to feed the hungry, they had begun to understand that, so long as an Indian could procure food at their doors, he would not seek it elsewhere for himself. They feared to anger the Indians by refusal and yet, as will appear later, their own storehouse was not over-crowded with food and they were already beginning to fear that a shortage would come upon them, before their harvests should come in. They made themselves friendly with the Indians whom they met, however, and were by them escorted to the village. Here they were entertained in a friendly manner. Food was set before them, consisting of the spawn of shad caught in the river and a cake made of crushed corn which they called maizium. This was doubtless the Rhode Island johnny-cake, that has persevered to this day.

After the envoys had eaten, they entertained their Indian hosts with some specimens of their skill with the gun, killing a crow at eighty yards, which greatly amazed and awed the beholders. Since Pokanoket, the seat of Massasoit, was still too far distant for a day's journey, the envoys and their guide presently set out again on their long walk and made eight miles farther before sunset. On the banks of the River Titicut, a branch of the Taunton, they found a party of Indians fishing for bass, as Winslow records, but which were probably shad. They bartered some of their own food for some of the fish and when night came slept in the open field. Doubtless they found their bivouac far more comfortable than had been those on the extremity of Cape Cod, in the preceding November.

After a night's rest the party resumed its journey, accompanied by half a dozen Indians who had joined themselves to the company. They were obliged to cross at two or three fords, at one of which passes they were attacked by two aged Indians, who supposed them to be enemies. But no harm was done to any one upon either side. The envoys, with the aid of Squanto, were able to pronounce their shibboleth aright and none fell in the encounter. The region through which they were obliged to pass was, of course, wild country, without roads and often thickly grown with trees and undergrowth. But they often came upon clearings, where evidently human beings had lived, for there were traces of cornfields, and now and then the unburied remains of those who had died in the great plague which had swept over this region. They encountered Indians singly and in groups, both men and women, in their long tramp and met with many adventures, but were treated with kindness by all. They often bestowed little gifts upon those whom they met, as evidences of their own good will.

It was late in the day on Tuesday when they came to the village where lived the great sagamore Massasoit. This was not far from the site of the present town of Warren, in Rhode Island. When they arrived Massasoit was absent, but he was sent for in great haste and reached home the next day. He welcomed his palefaced guests warmly and they in turn delivered to him a message from the governor of Plymouth. With this message was given a present of an English hunting coat of red cotton cloth, ornamented with lace, in which the sachem hastened to array himself. The envoys then placed about his neck a chain, or collar, of bright copper, which still more delighted the savage chieftain. The message of the governor conveyed many assurances of his good will toward his friend Massasoit and protested his desire to live peaceably with all men and especially with his nearest neighbors. Very delicately Governor Bradford intimated that, while he would always be glad to receive a visit from King Massasoit, he regretted that the shortness of their own provisions and the uncertainty of their first harvest forbade the entertainment of many of his subjects. He suggested that the colonists would always be glad to purchase skins of the Indians. He then alluded to the subject of the corn which the people had found buried at Pamet, on Cape Cod, and asked that Massasoit would kindly ascertain who were its rightful owners, that he might repay to them its value. Lastly, Governor Bradford, having learned that the Indians at Pokanoket had corn of a variety different from that which they had found at Cape Cod, desired of Massasoit that he would exchange for some of their corn, that he might experiment with the seed to ascertain which agreed best with the soil at Plymouth.

Massasoit replied to this address, bidding them welcome; assuring them that the peace made with them should continue and that his men should no more annoy the colonists; promising to send to Pamet and fix the ownership of the borrowed corn, and promising also to meet their wishes in the matter of seed corn. Nothing could have been more genial than this welcome of the Indian chief to the white invader of his country. He made a great speech to the men of his tribe, who gathered about him, enforcing upon them the idea of keeping a lasting peace with the white men. But although the Indian welcome was so genial and so glad were they to receive this visit from the white brothers, yet no invitation came to sup with them. Pipes and tobacco were offered, but no preparations were made for supper, and, indeed, bedtime came and all went fasting to bed.

It was a comfortless night which the two envoys passed. The bed was of planks, raised but a foot from the ground and covered with only a thin mat. The bed was uncomfortably crowded too, for several of the chief men of the tribe, besides the king himself, crowded into the narrow quarters. There were other companions, also, invisible, but no less attentive. The air swarmed with mosquitoes, and to their songs was added the monotonous droning of the Indians, who took this method of wooing sleep. Of course, under such conditions, there was but little sleep for the two white men. The next day many lesser chiefs came to pay their respects to the envoys and there were some games, but still no food was offered them. The truth was that they were out of provisions and game was scarce. The visitors had come in an unfortunate time, and they presently discovered that their condition was a cause of great mortification to the king and to all his people, who were naturally very hospitable. For nearly two days no food was brought into the village, save two large fishes, and these must be divided among forty people.

On the fourth day after their departure from Plymouth they set out on the return journey, faint for lack of food. Distresed at his seeming inhospitality, Massasoit detailed one of his men, named Tokamahamon, to accompany them and assist Squanto in procuring food by the way. But little food was found, however, and finally a messenger was sent before them to Plymouth, with the request that food be sent to them at Namasket, where they might find it when they should reach that village. The next night they were drenched with rain, a sudden thunder storm coming up, so that when they finally reached home, late Saturday night, they were wet, weary, and footsore, but rejoicing.

This notable journey was soon followed by another, in the opposite direction and for a far different reason. Among the families of the Pilgrim company was one which was little credit to them. This was the family of one John Billington, who were of the party which came down from London and joined the company at Southampton. Nothing is known of Billington previous to his joining the company. Bradford says of this family that "he and some of his had been often punished for miscarriages, being one of the profanest families amongst them. They came from London and I know not by what friends shuffled into their company." While the Mayflower lay at Cape Cod one of the boys of the Billington family, while playing with his father's gun in the cabin, discharged the piece, in close proximity to an open keg of powder. Only the Lord's mercy saved the ship and the entire company from being blown to pieces. Within a year after the settlement at Plymouth the elder Billington was the first to commit an offense in the colony. "For contempt of the captain's lawful command, with opprobrious speeches, he was adjudged to have his neck and heels tied together." Ten years after, Billington had the distinction of being the first of the colony to be hanged.

But to return to our story. Scarcely had the embassy to King Massasoit returned home, when the same boy who performed the exploit with the gun straggled away and "lost himselfe in the woods and wandered up and down some five days, living on berries and what he could find." The colony was, of course, aroused and a searching party was organized. The Indians of the Cape region were communicated with, and at length a trace of the boy was found. He had wandered away many miles down the Cape, penetrating even to the region of the Nauset Indians, the very tribe which had attacked the exploring party some months before. The shallop was manned and an expedition proceeded to Nauset, where the missing boy was found. He had been treated with great kindness by the Indians, who brought him on their shoulders through the shallow waters to the shallop and surrendered him to the searching party, adorned with necklaces of beads made from shells. The exploit of the boy was no doubt a cause of great exasperation to the people of the colony, who were thereby put to much anxiety and inconvenience.

The expedition to Nauset, however, was productive of much good. The colonists learned that the attack made upon their exploring party had been in consequence of some depredations which the Indians had suffered, some time previously, from the crew of a French vessel, which had landed on the coast. The Indians had supposed, naturally enough, that they were to suffer further depredations from this newly arrived party, whose movements they had been closely watching. More than this, the colonists found the owner of the corn which they had taken and gave him full satisfaction therefor, much to the delight of the Indians. The irritation felt at the carelessness and stupidity of the Billington boy was greatly tempered by the good which had ensued.

The excitement incident to this occurrence had scarcely abated when a fresh cause of trouble arose. About this time an Indian named Hobamack had attached himself to the colony. He was, says Bradford, "a proper lustie man and a man of accounte for his valour and parts amongst the Indians, and continued very faithful and constant to the English till he dyed." Hobamack and Squanto had been sent upon an expedition, perhaps for trade, to the Indians, when they were attacked by an inferior chief called Corbitant, who drew a knife and threatened to kill Hobamack. As it appeared some time later, this Corbitant was jealous of Massasoit and hoped to supplant him as sachem. He was therefore jealous of the whites as well and sought a cause of quarrel. As before noted, the Pilgrims early discerned the Indian character and saw that, should they show the slightest trace of fear in their dealings with the natives, they would lay themselves open to liability of attack. It was therefore determined to deal vigorously with this feint of Corbitant's, and at once, without the slightest hesitation or delay, the colony's first military expedition was hastily formed.

Standish, who had been elected the military commander of the colony, formed a company of fourteen men, brave and well-armed. With Hobamack as their guide they set out, with instructions, if Squanto should have been killed, to bring back with them the head of Corbitant. This expedition set out on the 14th of August. The story of their exploit is graphic. Stealing in Indian fashion silently through the woods, they surrounded the Indian village, the home of Corbitant, gave a sudden signal of attack, threw firebrands over the stockade which surrounded the wigwams, guarded the exits, and, as the Indians rushed out, attacked them as they fled. The suddenness and boldness of the attack thoroughly frightened the Indians, who at once offered to make peace. Corbitant chanced to be absent and so escaped the attack, but the lesson was to him just as severe as if he had been present. "After this," says Bradford, "they had many gratulations from diverce sachems and much firmer peace."

A few weeks later, an exploring expedition discovered Boston Bay and they returned "wishing they had been there seated. But it seems the Lord," adds Bradford, "who assignes to all men the bounds of their habitations, had appoynted it for another use." "And thus they found the Lord," he continues, "to be with them in all their ways and to bless their outgoings and incomings, for which let His holy name have the praise forever, to all posteritie." During this expedition they landed upon a rocky promontory, not far from the site of the present village of Neponset, which, in honor of their Indian guide they called Squantum; and Squantum it is to this day.

Autumn was now upon them and they began to gather their small harvests. All were now in good health, and although the harvest was not abundant, the fishing was excellent. Game was also plentiful. There was "great store of wild turkeys," besides venison and ducks and geese in good numbers. They now began to feel that their troubles were well-nigh over. One day in November some upon the shore descried a small white spot far out at sea, close to the horizon. Breathlessly they watched until it grew larger and larger and presently they made certain that a vessel was approaching, but whether of friend or foe they knew not. Greater grew the company of watchers upon the shore. Some ran to arms lest the coming ship might be an enemy. But soon they knew that it was no enemy ship which was approaching, for when she entered the harbor and dropped anchor before the little village, they learned that it was the Fortune, bringing reinforcements for the colony. The party comprised thirty-five persons, "most of them lusty young men," who were a welcome addition to the colony. They had, however, come out poorly fitted for the new life, lacking suitable clothing and totally lacking provisions. "The plantation was glad of this addition," says Bradford, "but could have wished that many of them had been of better condition."

The newcomers before their arrival had heard nothing of the ill fortune which had attended the Mayflower expedition; indeed, they had expected to find the settlement at Cape Cod, for some fleeting rumor seems to have reached England, doubtless through the crew of the Mayflower, that they had made a landing at that place. But the Fortune was at once laden with beaver and other skins, salted fish, and other commodities, consigned to the Merchant Adventurers, and in a short two weeks' time the ship left on her homeward voyage, leaving the colonists, as it will later appear, again to struggle against grim adversity.

XI

TROUBLOUS TIMES IN PLYMOUTH

THE coming of the Fortune brought good cheer to the infant colony at Plymouth, in that their losses by death were in a measure repaired by the coming of reinforcements from Leyden. But the Fortune brought also a disheartening and insulting message from Weston, who represented the Merchant Adventurers. This letter was addressed to Governor Carver, who, as we know, had died of sunstroke the previous spring. He took the colonists severely to task because they had allowed the Mayflower to return empty. "That you sent no lading in the ship is wonderful," he wrote, "and worthily distasted. I know your weakness was the cause of it, and I believe more weakness of judgment than weakness of hands. A quarter of the time you spent in discoursing, arguing and consulting would have done much more." To receive such a letter would have been a serious blow to the sweet-spirited and dignified Carver, but he had long been beyond the reach of such exhibitions of spleen. Bradford replied in a calm tone, informing Weston of the disasters which had well-nigh overwhelmed the colony. "Now to be so greatly blamed for not freighting the ship," he remonstrated, "doth indeed goe near us and much discourage us." Of Weston and his character we shall hear more later.

As we know, the Fortune was sent home with a valuable cargo of beaver skins and other commodities to the value of about twenty-five hundred dollars, which they believed would go far toward liquidating their indebtedness to the Merchant Adventurers. The result, however, added to the discouragement of the colonists, for the Fortune was captured by French pirates and her entire cargo stolen.

The work of lading the vessel being completed, and the Fortune dispatched on her return voyage, the colonists began to prepare for the coming winter. It was now November, just one year since they sighted Cape Cod and dropped anchor in Provincetown harbor. The additions to their number had brought the colony numerically nearly back to its original size, and their first thought was of their provisions for the winter which was before them. It must have been with a shudder that they recalled the horrors of the first winter, and it must have been with apprehension that they counted the number of mouths which must be filled and contemplated the slender supply of corn in their granary. Now it was that they realized as never before the goodness of that Providence which had revealed to them the store of hidden corn, on the hill slope on the far tip of Cape Cod. For when their harvest was gathered they found that the seed which they had brought with them from England had come to naught, and had not this native corn been found by them, and served them for seed, the colony could not have survived the second winter, but must inevitably have perished from hunger.

But the autumn gave great promise of abundance. Although their barley and peas had been a disappointment, their harvest of corn "did prove well and, God be praised! we had a good increase of Indian corn." So wrote Edward Winslow to a friend in England. And so the colonists bethought them of the necessity of thankfulness, and they resolved to return thanks for their harvest. And so was established in Plymouth the first New England Thanksgiving Day. The governor "sent four men on fowling" and the four in one day "killed as much fowl as, with a little help besides, served the company almost a week." To join them in their festival King Massasoit visited them, with a retinue of ninety men "whom for three days we entertained and feasted." The Indians killed five deer, which they brought as their contribution to the feast, and there were wild turkeys and ducks and geese in abundance, so that there was a great rejoicing among them.

But after the harvest festival was over and the cold weather approached, the governor and his assistant realized that the present time was none too early to make a careful computation of the length of time which their store of provisions would last. Therefore they "tooke an exacte accounte of all their provisions in store and proportioned the same to the number of persons and found that it would not hold out above six months at half allowance, and hardly that." In other words gaunt famine was staring them in the face. The Fortune had brought thirty-five colonists, but not a pound of provisions with which to feed them through the winter. At once the entire colony was placed upon half allowance. This deprivation of sufficient food soon "begane to be hard, but they bore it patiently under hope of supply." But no supply came to them. As the cold of winter began to grip them the game which had been so plentiful in woods, in marshes, and along the shore rapidly disappeared. It is true there was fish in the sea; winter is the harvest time for the Cape Cod fisherman of to-day. But the gear which they had brought with them was sadly inadequate. Even the fish hooks which they had brought were of unsuitable size, and although fish in great numbers were near them, they were unable to take many. The lobsters, which they had taken in great quantities during the summer, had all disappeared, for in cold weather the lobster creeps away into deep water, where the frost does not penetrate.

The winter wore away, the entire company on half rations; but as spring opened food grew still more scarce. The supply of corn rapidly became exhausted and at last all was gone save that which was religiously reserved for seed, and the colonists were obliged to rely upon what the country afforded, for their sustenance. "In these straits," wrote Winslow, "such was our state as, in the morning, we had often our food to seek for the day and yet performed the duties of our callings. And though at times, in some seasons, at noon I have seen men stagger, by reason of faintness for want of food, yet ere night, by the good Providence and blessing of God, we have enjoyed such plenty as though the windows of heaven had been opened unto us." Throughout all this lack these people never for a moment lost their faith, nor their gratitude. Elder Brewster, we are told, when often he sat down to a repast of clams, with a cup of cold water, looked up to heaven and returned thanks "for the abundance of the sea and for the treasures hid in the sand." When the spring had sufficiently opened for planting they went into their fields and loosened the soil and planted the scanty store of seed corn which they had saved even in their hunger and extremity, for they well saw the necessity of providing for another year's harvest.

Scarcely had the fresh young shoots begun to appear, when a messenger came to them from Canonicus, sachem of the Narragansetts, who inhabited the region on the west side of the bay, to which has been given the name of that tribe. The message boded no good to the colonists, for it was a challenge to war. In his hand the messenger bore a bundle of arrows, tied about with the skin of a rattlesnake. Once more the colonists faced a most serious problem; but the idea of Standish, that the attitude of the colonists toward aggressive Indians must be fearless, was undoubtedly the only course safe to pursue in such emergencies. Without an instant of hesitation Standish took the bundle of arrows, removed the rattlesnake's skin, filled it with powder and shot and returned it to the messenger with a bold answer. The fearlessness of the colonists had its effect upon Canonicus, and so thoroughly frightened was the savage chief that he refused to receive the snake-skin, with its contents. It passed from hand to hand and at last found its way back to Plymouth. The bold answer was sufficient, for nothing more was heard from the threatening Narragansetts. As a precautionary measure the colonists inclosed their village with a stockade of logs and for a long time mounted guards at the gates day and night. But no enemy came upon them.

THE MAYFLOWER PILGRIMS

Near the end of May, 1622, when their store of provisions had become nearly exhausted, a small sailing vessel was seen approaching Plymouth. A fresh trouble had come upon them. They had hoped that they had heard their last of Thomas Weston, but he was destined for a long time to be to them a thorn in the flesh. In this little vessel came seven men as passengers and a letter from Weston, in which he announced that he was planning to establish a colony on his own account, at some place not far distant from Plymouth. The seven men were the advance guard of a larger number, who were to come. A larger vessel, he said, would soon arrive at Plymouth, with a considerable number of settlers, whom the Plymouth people were coolly asked to entertain until the new colony should be established.

Weston was as good as his word. This advance party had been sent forward from Monhegan, the English fishing station on the Maine coast. Not long after, another party arrived and sixty more men, whom Weston himself called "rude fellows," were dumped upon Plymouth, for the colonists to feed and lodge, for an indefinite period. The vessel which brought this motley crew sailed away to Virginia and the colonists were obliged to feed nearly seventy unwelcome men from their scanty stores. Some of the newcomers became ill and must be cared for. "But of their victuals they had not any," wrote Bradford, "though they were in great wante, nor anything else in recompense of any courtesy done them." They were "an unruly company," says Bradford, and their coming reduced the colony to still greater straits. They succeeded, however, in procuring some provisions from Monhegan. As their corn began to ear, these "rude fellows" made themselves free in the colonists' cornfields. They soon discovered the excellent qualities of ears of green corn roasted before the fire and although some of them were well flogged for thus meddling with the harvests, even this did not deter them from repeating the offense.

After spending the entire summer as unbidden guests of the Plymouth people, Weston's party made a settlement at a place called Wessagusset, not far from the spot where now is the great plant of the Fore River Shipbuilding Company. They built a few log huts and essayed to make there a settlement. But no women were of the company and hence there were no homemakers. They were an improvident gang of roysterers, whose sole thought was of the day. Unable to procure provisions, they suggested to the Plymouth people that they should jointly make an expedition along the coast for the purchase of corn from the natives. The Plymouth people accepted the suggestion; and taking the vessel of the new settlers, which had now returned from Virginia, they set out upon the journey. They were successful in obtaining several hogsheads of corn, which was divided between the two settlements. This welcome addition to their store was of great advantage to the Plymouth people, for their harvest had been none too large. But the improvident fellows at Wessagusset soon dissipated their share, making no effort to find food from woods or shore until their last handful of corn was gone. Then they resorted to begging and stealing from the Indians, until the natives about them became disgusted and incensed. The result of the misbehavior of this gang was the formation of a widespread conspiracy among the Indians of the entire region, in which a plan was laid to exterminate, not alone the men of Wessagusset, but also the entire colony of Plymouth.

The misbehavior of one company of white men had disgusted the natives with white men in general; and had the conspiracy succeeded, every paleface on the New England coast would have been massacred, even as a large number of whites had shortly before been massacred in a Virginia settlement. Every tribe in the region, save the Wampanoags, was concerned in this conspiracy. But Massasoit had made a treaty with Plymouth and he kept his faith with his white brothers.

At about this time it was learned at Plymouth that Massasoit was exceedingly ill, perhaps unto death. Winslow at once headed a relief party and, with the aid of such rude medical skill as he had acquired, he succeeded in saving the life of the sachem. The Indian Hobamack, who had accompanied Winslow on his journey, disclosed to him, as they were returning, the secret of the conspiracy, which had been confided to him by Massasoit. Plymouth was thus warned of the plan of massacre and was able to forestall the movement.

The Plymouth people had already surmised that something serious was impending, but the great extent of the conspiracy they had not suspected. In the meantime the men of Wessagusset had reached serious straits for lack of food, this condition being due wholly to their improvidence and to Weston's neglect to supply his colony with provisions. Some of the company actually perished of cold and hunger, and the Indians openly scorned and insulted them and would even come into the settlement and seize food which the white men had cooked for their own eating. At this juncture Weston appeared at Plymouth, in great need, and succeeded in borrowing one hundred beaver skins from the settlers, which he never returned nor paid for. He then disappeared, giving no aid to his starving colonists at Wessagusset. The Wessagusset men now disclosed to Plymouth a plan which they had formed of a forcible robbery of the Indians' store of corn. Against such a procedure the Plymouth colonists strenuously objected.

Meanwhile the attitude of the Indians toward both the colony at Wessagusset and that at Plymouth rapidly became more aggressive. Phineas Pratt, of Wessagusset, escaped from that settlement and made his way through the woods, a twenty-five-mile journey, to Plymouth, to warn the people of that settlement that he feared an Indian attack upon both colonies. The intelligence which he brought tallied well with the warnings given by Massasoit.

Now comes into the story the bad Indian Wituwamat, who has been mentioned in a previous chapter. Not long before this time, Standish had visited the sachem Canacum at Manomet, for the purpose of purchasing corn. Wituwamat made his appearance in the Indian village, and in the presence of Standish made a wild harangue to the Indians. Standish was able to understand enough of the talk to comprehend that danger threatened the white colonies. The time for action was becoming ripe. Massasoit had urged his white friends to strike first, strike suddenly, and strike hard, if they would avert a general massacre of white settlers. Standish at once summoned his brave army of ten and took up his march for Wessagusset.

Reaching that settlement, they found its people well scattered and demoralized. Wituwamat, big, powerful, and boastful, was there and with him another Indian as large and powerful as himself, called Pecksuot. Both were brandishing their knives in the faces of Standish and his men and uttering taunts and threats against the white men. Standish was a man of small stature, and this fact excited the derision of the two braves and called forth their louder taunts. The two Indians, who were the leaders of a concealed horde longing for blood, were induced to enter one of the log houses of the settlement, where were Standish and four or five of his men. Suddenly, at a slight signal, the whites made an onslaught upon their Indian foes. Standish rushed upon Pecksuot, snatched the savage's own knife from his neck where it hung and with it slew the Indian braggart. Wituwamat at the same instant was attacked by the other whites of the party and in a few moments both Indians were slain. So sudden was the onslaught that the two Indians, although they resisted stoutly, could do little to defend themselves. The effect upon the followers of the two conspirators and upon the Indian tribes along the coast, even to Martha's Vineyard and Cape Cod, was efficacious. Instantly was the widespread conspiracy shattered. Tribes from far and near hastened to offer peace to the Plymouth colonists. Not long after this occurrence the Wessagusset colonists, thoroughly discouraged, embarked in their vessel and sailed away toward the

Maine coast. They were never again heard of to vex the Plymouth settlers.

Pastor Robinson at Leyden was greatly disturbed when the story of this encounter with the savages reached his ears. "How happy a thing had it been," he wrote to the colonists, "if you had converted some before you killed any; besides, where blood is once begun to be shed it is seldom staunched of a long time after." But Pastor Robinson knew nothing of the widespread conspiracy which threatened to cut off the entire colony of Plymouth, men, women, and children, at a blow, and he had no conception whatever of the Indian character. Doubtless the stern necessity of following the advice of their friend Massasoit, as the only measure of safety, was as serious a matter of regret to Bradford and Brewster as it was, afterward, to Robinson. But necessity knows no law. If they would preserve their own lives and those of their wives and children, they must strike swiftly and suddenly; and the blow was given, and given with energy and efficiency. Myles Standish took his life in his hands in this bold encounter; but he was preserved from harm, and the Plymouth Colony was once more delivered from the hand of the spoiler.

XII

FAMINE AGAIN ASSAILS PLYMOUTH

THE famine which beset the people of Plymouth in the first year of their settlement was not their only struggle with the gaunt wolf of hunger. We have already read of the coming of the Fortune and the addition which it brought to the number of the colonists, and of the coming also of the Weston settlers, who were dumped upon the people of Plymouth, greatly to their distress. We have learned that the magistrates, who fortunately controlled the food supply, placed all upon half allowance. So short, indeed, was the supply of food that at one time the people of the colony were restricted each to a quarter of a pound of bread daily. But their faith was perfect, and when the hour was darkest and when the food was wholly exhausted, a fresh supply came from unexpected sources, so that they passed through their days of trial and none died of hunger.

In the autumn came their harvest, but, Bradford writes: "It arose but to a little in comparison of a full year's supply, partly by reason they were not yet well acquainted with the manner of Indian corn, also their many other employments, but chiefly their weakness for want of food, to tend it as they should have done." Not this alone, but it will be recalled that the Weston party made free with the roasting ears, so that the fields were sadly depleted. So small was the long expected harvest that "it well appeared that famine must still ensue the next year also, if not some way prevented."

At this juncture an English trading ship came into the harbor, "one Captain Jones being chief therein." From this ship the Plymouth colonies secured a supply of beads and knives, for use in trade with the natives. Captain Jones, seeing their need, drove a hard bargain with them, but, even at the exorbitant rates which were demanded, the colonists were glad to procure these fresh supplies for barter, for this meant an ability to buy a fresh corn supply, when their greatest need should come.

In the spring of 1623, so great had been the discontent over the strict communistic system of planting and harvesting, after much debate "the governor gave way that they should set corn every man for his own particular and in that regard trust to themselves." Each family was assigned a parcel of land for planting, and all went to work with renewed interest and diligence. This new plan met with great success, so that even the women of the families gladly went into the cornfields to help in the planting and hoeing, taking their little children along with them, that they might care for them while they themselves worked. All this was done eagerly and willingly, although before this to have compelled these women to perform such tasks would have been regarded as tyranny and oppression.

But while these crops were growing, before harvest time came again they found their food supply exhausted, and Bradford says, "they were only to rest on God's providence, at night not many times knowing where to have anything the next day, and so, as one well observed, had need to pray that God would give them their daily bread above all people in the world."

In their extremity they turned to the sea. They had but a single boat suitable for fishing, "and she not over well fitted." They had but a single small seine and but few fishhooks and these too large for their purpose. They divided the men of the colony into companies of six or seven men, each to take its regular turn at fishing. It was made a rule that when one company went out it was not to return without a fare of fish. It was not uncommon, under this rule, for a party to be absent for a number of days together, especially in heavy weather, a circumstance which doubtless occasioned much anxiety among those at home. Upon the return of one party the next in order at once manned the vessel and started out, so that the colony's labor in fishing was unceasing. "If she stayed long or got little," says Bradford, "then all went to seeking of shelfish, which at low water they digged out of the sands. And this was their living in the summertime till God sent them better, and in winter they were helped with ground nuts and fowl. Also in the summer they got now and then a deer, for one or two of the fittest was appointed to range the woods for that end, and what was got that way was divided amongst them."

In May, 1623, came upon them a fresh discouragement. As we know, they had planted an unusual crop of corn and there was such enthusiasm in the caring for it that even the women and children went into the fields for the hoeing. But presently the growth of the young plants was checked by a great drought, "insomuch as the corne begane to wither away, though it was set with fish, the moysture whereof helped it much. Yet at length it begane to languish sore, and some of the drier grounds were parched like withered hay. Upon which they sett aparte a solemn day of humiliation, to seeke the Lord by humble and fervente prayer in this great distress. And He was pleased to give them a gracious and speedy answer, both to their own and the Indians' admiration, that lived amongst them. For all the morning and greatest part of the day it was clear weather and very hot and not a cloud or any signe of raine to be seen, yet toward evening it begane to overcast and shortly after to raine, with such sweete and gentle showers as gave them cause of rejoicing and blessing God. It came without either wind or thunder or any violence and by degrees in that abundance as that the earth was thoroughly wet and soaked therewith; which did so apparently revive and quicken the decayed corn and other fruits, as was wonderful to see and made the Indians astonished to behold. And afterward the Lord sent them such seasonable showers, with interchange of fair, warm weather, as through His blessing caused a fruitful and liberal harvest, to their no small comforte and rejoycing." [1]

In the middle of June of this year the Pilgrims had yet another cause of great rejoicing. This was the coming of the ship called the Anne, which was soon followed by a smaller vessel called the Little James. By these ships came some whose arrival had been looked for and longed for by some of the first comers. Among these new arrivals were Patience and Fear Brewster, the daughters of Elder Brewster, and Barbara, whose other name we do not know, but who soon became the wife of Captain Myles Standish. By the Anne came also Alice Carpenter, the widow of Edward Southworth of Leyden, who soon after her arrival married Governor William Bradford. By this ship also came Manasseh and John Faunce, whose family name is perpetuated in that of the present president of a great New

[1] Bradford.

England college. In all, about sixty persons came by these ships to join themselves to the colony.

The story of the landing of this party at Plymouth and of their meeting with their friends who had preceded them, is pathetic in the extreme. "According to their diverse humores," says Bradford, they "were diversely affected." For when they looked upon their friends, the misery and distress of whose lives were fully shown forth in their countenances and in their dress, many burst into tears and wept and sobbed bitterly. "Many were ragged in apparel and some little better than half naked," says the record, and when they would call the newly arrived to refreshment, "the best dish they could presente their friends with was a lobster or a piece of fish, without bread or anything else but a cup of fair spring water."

Governor Bradford made his record of these events full thirty years after their occurrence, and yet so clearly were these distressing days fixed in his memory and so firm had been his faith, that he exclaims in his ecstasy: "But God fed them out of the sea, for the most part, so wonderful is His providence over His in all ages, for His mercie endureth forever."

When the Anne returned to England she went laden with a large quantity of beaver skins and other commodities, consigned to the Merchant Adventurers. With her went also Edward Winslow, "to informe of all things and procure such things as were thought needfull for their present condition."

And now the harvest, for which they had waited and striven, was come, and "instead of famine, now God gave them plentie and the face of things was changed, to the rejoysing of the hearts of many, for which they blessed God."

With the coming of the Anne a new element entered into the colony. With this ship, besides the sixty who were regarded as strictly members of the Plymouth Colony, were some who came, as it was expressed, "on their particular." That is, these came to become a part of the colony and yet not of it. These were, in character, far superior to the Weston party, of whom we have already heard; but they came with no intention of joining the community, but each designed to care for his own individual interests and to live, in a measure, apart from the colonial system. They, of course, saw the necessity of subjecting themselves to all wholesome laws made for the government of the colony and of joining, also, in all movements for the common defense. To these things they readily assented. They agreed, also, that each male above the age of sixteen should pay yearly a bushel of Indian corn, or its equivalent, into the common store; and they agreed, also, to abstain from all trade with the Indians until such time as the community system should be done away. The colonists, for their part, agreed to allot to them "competente places for habitations within the town" and to free them from such communistic employments as were required of the colonists themselves. The "particulars" were not to draw upon the common stock of food, nor were they to be required to share with the colonists the provisions which they brought with them.

These "particulars" were probably not wholly welcome, and their coming was certainly unexpected, but they were received "in all love and friendship," for they were perhaps in accord with the Plymouth colonists in matters of religion, and we learn of no considerable friction between the two classes of colonists.

In the autumn came a ship bearing Robert

Gorges, son of Sir Ferdinando Gorges, a member of the Council for New England, who brought "sundrie passengers and families," who designed to begin a plantation at some point about Massachusetts Bay. He and his party remained as rather unwelcome guests at Plymouth for a while, finally taking possession of the abandoned cabins at Wessagusset and making an attempt at colonization, which proved abortive. While this company was at Plymouth an event occurred which once more threatened to blot out the colony. This was a great fire, which broke out in the thatch of a cabin in Plymouth, in which some of the men of Gorges' ship's company were roystering. The fire spread rapidly to other dwellings and so to the near vicinity of the great common house, in which was stored their entire supply of provisions, including the corn lately harvested and their seed corn for the next year's planting.

The alarm and consternation which beset the little colony cannot adequately be described. We can imagine every colonist—men, women, and children—working heroically to save their town from utter destruction. Both within and without the common house they fought the fire as best they could, "with wet cloths and other means," so that "through God's mercie it was saved by the great diligence of the people."

As a result of this fire a number of the "particulars" abandoned their plans of colonization and returned to England, some because of "discontente and dislike of the country," and others by reason of the loss of their provisions by the fire. And so this new feature in the colony ceased to be a disturbing factor. We hear little more of the "particulars," and when, a few years later, the communistic system was abolished, the distinction between the two classes of colonists disappeared.

An incident of the brief incursion of the Gorges company into the country must not be omitted. With this party came a clergyman of the Church of England, named Morell. When the Gorges company abandoned its attempt at settlement and returned to England, Mr. Morell remained and with a few companions lingered for a year longer in the nearly deserted cabins at Wessagusset. He passed the time of his sojourn there in a quiet way, studying the animals, the trees and plants of that section and the habits and characteristics of the natives. During this time he composed a Latin poem, which has been preserved and together with a translation, is printed in one of the volumes of the collections of the Massachusetts Historical Society. In this poem he sings of the trees, plants, and flowers, of the beasts of the forest, and of the wild men of woods and plain.

In the spring of 1625 Mr. Morell went to Plymouth and there took ship for his return to England, and the colonists never saw him more. Before leaving, he disclosed to them a fact which, had it been before known, might have caused some uneasiness. He had brought with him a document from the Council for New England, granting to him full authority of superintendency over the religious affairs of the colony. In other words, his commission gave him full power to enforce upon the Plymouth Church conformity to the Church of England. Mr. Morell had, however, kept his commission a secret until he was upon the point of departure, and hence had, of course, made no attempt to enforce his authority upon them. Mr. Adams[1] remarks that "a priest of another

---

[1] Charles Francis Adams: Three Episodes of Massachusetts History, I. 156.

description would almost assuredly have proved a mischief-maker." As it was, Mr. Morell had been wholly inoffensive in his attitude toward Plymouth, but after his disclosure of his paper authority over their worship, it is probable that the colonists did not grieve at his going. Mr. Morell had been wise in not attempting to enforce his ecclesiastical authority, for the source of that authority was separated from him and them by three thousand miles of rough water and any such attempt must necessarily have been futile. But nevertheless the thought that an attempt even had been made, at this great distance, to enforce conformity upon them must have brought freshly to their minds some of the occurrences of their life in England and sent a shiver of dismay over them, at the thought that, after all their sufferings in the cause of conscience, the long arm of the law was still struggling to reach them. As we shall presently see, their misgivings were not wholly groundless.

XIII

PLYMOUTH ENCOUNTERS A URIAH HEEP

THE harvest of 1623, in the Plymouth Colony, which followed the prayers for rain, was the most abundant with which the colony had yet been favored and "instead of famine now God gave them plentie," and from that day forth no want or famine came upon them. As we already know, the Anne was speedily laden with beaver skins and other commodities, which were soon dispatched to England with the fervent hope of the colonists that the vessel would not meet with the fate which befell the Fortune.

It will be remembered that with the return of the ship to England had gone Edward Winslow on business for the colony. His return in one respect marked a significant era in the history of Plymouth Colony. John Fiske, in his Discovery of America,[1] holds it to be

[1] I. 218.

"difficult to imagine a community of Euro-
peans subsisting anywhere for any length of
time without domestic animals"; and he re-
gards the absence of domestic animals among
the North American Indians as very important among the causes which retarded the prog-
ress of mankind in this part of the world. With
the return of Winslow the colony entered upon
what Fiske calls the pastoral stage of development in civilization, and this development in
Plymouth Colony was rapid. Early in 1624
came the ship Charity, in which Mr. Winslow
returned to Plymouth, bringing with him, for
the use of the colony, a small number of cattle,
which became the nucleus of a considerable
herd. The results of this addition to the re-
sources of the colony were incalculable.

On the Charity came also one John Lyford,
a clergyman of the Church of England, described as of Puritan tendencies. It is not impossible that Dickens, in David Copperfield,
if perchance he was versed in Pilgrim history,
may have drawn from the character of Lyford
what the novelist denominates "that crawling
impersonation of meanness, Uriah Heep." He
certainly strongly resembled that notable character, in his affectation of extreme humility,

upon his arrival in Plymouth Colony. "'Umble we are, 'umble we have been, 'umble we shall ever be," said Mrs. Heep, speaking of herself and of her son Uriah; and when Lyford first came ashore, Bradford tells us, "he saluted them with that reverence and humilitie as is seldome to be seen, and, indeed, made them ashamed, he so bowed and cringed unto them and would have kissed their hands if they would have suffered him; yea, he wept and shed many tears, blessing God that had brought him to see their faces and admiring the things they had done in their wants, as if he had been made all of love and the humblest person in the world. And all the while, if we may judge by his after carriage, he was but like him mentioned in Psalms X, 10, that croucheth and boweth that heaps of poore may fall by his might."

Lyford was received with unusual kindness and was given the best entertainment possible and a larger allowance of food out of the storehouse than was granted to others. More than this, Governor Bradford, who had been accustomed to consult with Elder Brewster in all weighty public matters, now called Lyford also into his councils. Presently Lyford made known his desire to unite with the Plymouth church, and he was accordingly received on confession of faith.

A momentary digression must here be made in the narrative, to bring into the story the name of one John Oldham, who was of the party who came in the Anne, "on their particular," as noted in a previous chapter. It had become known to the colonists that some person among the "particulars" had written to the Council for New England a letter, in which various complaints were lodged against the colonists, apparently for the purpose of arraying the council against them. There was reason to believe that the author of these calumnies was Oldham. Indeed, after the coming of Lyford, for whom he soon evinced a warm friendship, Oldham humbly confessed that "he had done them wrong by word and deed and writing into England, but he now saw the eminent hand of God to be with them, and his blessing upon them, which made his heart smite him; neither should those in England ever use him as an instrumente any longer against them in anything."

Thus Bradford tells us, all things "seemed to go very comfortably and smoothly, at which they did much rejoice." But this condition did not long prevail, and soon it became evident that both Lyford and Oldham were attempting to form factions and stir up strife among the colonists, while maintaining a pretense of great friendliness and brotherly kindness toward them. Both Bradford and Brewster were men not easily hoodwinked, and while they accepted in all good graces the protestations of friendliness made by this pair of undoubted spies, they kept their eyes sharply about them. Presently a ship was about to sail for England and, as the crew was making ready for her departure, it was observed that both Lyford and Oldham were devoting themselves closely to literary labors. There were many secret whisperings between the two and many sly winks passed, which they evidently believed to be unnoticed. But Governor Bradford was quietly observant of all that was passing and he had already had experience with Oldham as a foreign correspondent.

It was not unusual, when a vessel sailed for the homeland, for some of the chief men of the colony to accompany it down the bay in the shallop. Sometimes it happened that there were unfinished letters, which it was important should be sent by the ship, and by this means an opportunity was offered to complete them. When, therefore, Governor Bradford accompanied this ship down the bay, in the shallop, no surprise was felt; and when he quietly returned to the town, after a few hours at sea, of course no questions were asked, nor suspicions excited. In fact, the vessel set sail near evening, taking advantage doubtless of the late tide, and since the governor's return was delayed until after nightfall, his homecoming attracted no notice.

Not long after the departure of this vessel, Lyford, together with a few whom he had succeeded in drawing about him—Oldham being of the number—attempted to create a schism in the Plymouth church and to effect, by revolution, the establishment of the very form of worship which they had left England to escape. In short, Lyford was an emissary of the English Establishment, who had come out for the purpose of creating a faction, which should overthrow independence in religion and again force upon them conformity to the established system. In other words, the very thing which they had left England to escape was reaching out after them in their new home in the wilderness, and the danger seemed imminent that all the troubles and distresses which had beset them would be for naught. Presently Oldham fell into open revolt against the civil authority, refusing to serve his turn with others at the watch and assailing Standish with fierce denunciations, even drawing a knife in a threatening manner. Evidently, open rebellion in the colony was imminent. Oldham was placed under arrest and confined for a while, but the governor feared that more active measures than this were necessary to insure the peace of the colony.

In order to bring the matter to a crisis, Governor Bradford presently called a town meeting, to consider some matters of general interest to the colony. When all were assembled in the common house, the governor presented the subject of the discords which were afflicting the community and most of all deprecated the disaffections apparent among some. Warming to his subject, Governor Bradford openly charged the two men, Lyford and Oldham, with spreading disaffection among the people and with plotting against the stability of the colony and disturbing their peace both in civil and religious affairs. Lyford, the governor declared, had come over in a vessel sent at the expense of the colony and he and his family had been received with all kindness and had been maintained at the public charge. But now, the governor charged, he was plotting against them and seeking their ruin. As for Oldham, he had, it was true, come on his own "particular," but he had been well received and treated with all courtesy; but now he, too, was doing his utmost to injure the colony and defeat the ends for which the colonists had come hither.

These abrupt and searching charges, boldly made in open meeting, were received with astonishment by the people and with affected indignation by Lyford and Oldham. The two men volubly denied the governor's charges. Lyford especially declared openly that he had held no communication whatever with people in England, concerning matters in the colony. When the two had ceased their indignant denials, there was a moment of tense silence, followed by a dramatic incident. Governor Bradford quietly reached for a packet of papers, which had until then lain unnoticed and unremarked, and amid breathless stillness selected one and began to read. It was a letter written by Lyford to parties in England, filled with false accusations against the government of the colony and with cruel and unkind speeches concerning the colonists. Amid profound silence the governor read one letter after another, all of like tenor, some written by Lyford, others by Oldham, until the people were bursting with indignation. Governor Bradford, during his trip down the harbor, convoying the ship Charity, had taken the course still followed by nations in time of war or of great public stress. He had censored the mails. Some of Lyford's letters he had copied and forwarded the originals to their destination; but of those of the greatest moment he had forwarded the copies and retained the originals, so that the writer would find it impossible to deny their correctness.

Oldham interrupted the reading by a violent outburst and "began to rage furiously, because they had intercepted and opened his letters, threatening them in very high language." In a loud tone and in a mutinous manner he shouted and called upon those present, whom he believed to be his followers and supporters, to rise and show their courage in open revolt. But he called in vain, for none rushed to his standard. Lyford, for his part, was struck speechless at this revelation of his treachery, deceit, and falsehood. Among the recommendations which Lyford made in his letters were that no more of the Leyden people should be allowed to join the colony and especially that Pastor Robinson should at all hazards be prevented from coming; that a sufficient number of colonists should be sent over to "oversway" the original colonists; and that another should be sent to take the place of Captain Standish, who "looks like a silly boy." Lyford closed with the injunction: "I pray you conceal me in the discovery of these things."

When the governor had concluded the reading of the letters, he called upon Lyford to justify himself, if so it might be possible. He, stammering, attempted to cast the blame of the whole business upon Billington, but the latter denied any complicity in the matter and accused Lyford of attempting to draw him to a part with him in discord. At length Lyford broke down and resumed his character as Uriah Heep, and with abundant tears "confest he feared he was a reprobate, his sins were so great that he doubted God would not parden them," and much more to the same effect. By vote of the meeting the two men were expelled from the colony, but, not to be too severe, Oldham's wife and family were permitted to remain through the winter. Lyford was given a probationary period of six months, and before that time was passed, such were his protestations of repentance that the colonists were upon the point of rescinding their vote of expulsion. But just then he was discovered in the act of repeating the offense of which he had pretended so bitterly to repent.

A little later were made known some occurrences of Lyford's previous career, which seriously affected his moral character, and the sentence of expulsion was carried into effect. Lyford left the colony and dwelt for a time at Nantasket, where was a tiny settlement to which also Oldham had gone. Thence he drifted to Salem and afterward to Virginia, and Plymouth, much to its relief, knew him no more. But the colony did not soon recover from the effects of Lyford's presence among them. When Edward Winslow returned from England in the early part of 1625 he brought a communication from the Merchant Adventurers which clearly showed the hand of Lyford. This letter attacked the colonists upon religious grounds and threateneed a withdrawal of their financial support to the colony unless it should renounce what they called Brownism, or independence in religion. Not long after this, however, the Company of Merchant Adventurers disintegrated, and we do not learn that any attempt was actually made to carry into effect any of their threats against the colonists.

With the opening of the year 1624, it should be noted, as a matter of historical interest, came the annual election in the colony. Since now the number of colonists had considerably increased, it was determined that the governor who should be elected should be given five assistants, "for helpe and counsel," in place of one as heretofore. Later this number was increased to seven, this board of assistants, with the governor, being endowed with judicial as well as executive functions. This was the origin both of the present Governor's Council in Massachusetts and of the Supreme Court for the Commonwealth, as at present constituted.

It will perhaps be recalled that it was the intention of the Pilgrims, when they were planning to leave Leyden and emigrate to America, to maintain themselves by fishing, and that Sir Robert Naunton, when he broached to King James the plan of a settlement of religionists in the New World, was asked by the king how the proposed colony would maintain itself, and replied, "By fishing, your Majesty," to which the king responded: " 'Tis an honest trade. 'Twas the apostles' own calling." But, as we have learned, the fisheries of the colony were at first of no great moment and barely sufficed to supply the needs of the colonists themselves. But with the opening of the year 1624, with a full granary in the common house on the hill, the colonists began to bethink themselves of their original design of looking to the treasures of the sea, for commercial advantage and profit. There was still a large balance to their debit on the books of the Merchant Adventurers, who had financed the voyage of the Mayflower. Indeed, this debit remained against them for many years. It seemed to the colonists that to send goods to the Adventurers was much like pouring water into a sieve, and that the more the colony paid to the Adventurers, the greater was their debt. The Pilgrims, we must believe, were not acute financiers, and the Adventurers would seem to have often over-reached them in their dealings. Indeed, with the letter which attacked the religious features of the colony came another which announced that the amount still due the Adventurers from the colony was fourteen hundred pounds, or about seven thousand dollars, which amount must have seemed to them like a millstone about their necks.

But to return to the story of the fishing. Early in 1624 they determined to begin the business of fishing in earnest, and from this date may be reckoned the beginning of the vast fishing industry of Massachusetts, the only industry, save that of agriculture, which was thus established in the very earliest days of the Plymouth Colony and which has continued to flourish to the present time. It is the only industry in our land which has ever been the subject of diplomatic controversy with a European nation and which has been the subject of a separate and especial treaty. More than one hundred years ago the Great and General Court of Massachusetts, by an especial enactment, caused the effigy of a codfish to be hung in its Hall of Representatives, as typical of the importance of its fisheries to the people of the

State. This effigy of a codfish has been sacredly cared for and preserved and to the present day is a conspicuous object in the representatives' chamber in the State House at Boston.

A small vessel, called a pinnace, possibly the same vessel as that known as a shallop, was fitted out for fishing and, being well provisioned, was sent to the Maine coast. The first voyage was disastrous, for the boat was cast away in a storm and the captain was drowned. A year later a second attempt was made, which proved more successful. Convinced that an open boat was not suitable for fishing, especially in the winter time, they lengthened one of their shallops, decked her over and thus made a very suitable vessel for fishing, which answered their purpose for the next seven years. From this time forward the fisheries were doubtless the most important factor in the material prosperity of Plymouth Colony.

XIV

HAPPIER DAYS FOR PLYMOUTH

NEVER, it would seem, did any people who attempted to form a plantation in a new country, meet with such great vexations and discouragements as did the Pilgrims. And yet never did any show forth such boundless faith as did they. The latest of these discouraging affairs was the attempt of enemies in England, through Lyford and Oldham, to force upon them the form of religious worship to escape which they had passed through so great hardships and sufferings. This unpleasant affair over, the Pilgrim colony had reason to feel that their faith, tested to the utmost, had safely brought them through and set their feet firmly in the promised land. "It pleased the Lord," writes Bradford, "to give the plantation peace and health and contented minds and so to bless their labors, as they had corn sufficient and some to spare to others, with other foods. Neither ever had they any supply of food [from England] but what they first brought with them." The harvest of 1625 was still more abundant than that of the previous year, so that the colonists were able to send one of their small vessels, filled with the grain, "to the eastward, up a river called Kenibeck," where they bartered it to good advantage, for seven hundredweight of beaver skins, besides other furs. Truly the Pilgrim colony was beginning to be prosperous.

But yet the Company of Merchant Adventurers in London were still inclined to demand of the colonists their "pound of flesh." Veritable Shylocks, it would seem, were these men, who, defeated in their attempts at disturbing religious worship among these devoted people, seemed well determined to extort from them the uttermost farthing. Money for the use of the colony could be raised upon loan in London only at the most exorbitant rates of interest. Thirty, forty, and even fifty per cent was demanded by the rapacious London money-lenders. In the summer of 1625 two vessels came out from England on a fishing and trading voyage and the colonists took advantage of their return to dispatch Captain Standish to England. He bore letters and instructions to treat with the Merchant Adventurers and also with the Council for New England, to learn if it might not be possible to obtain goods upon sale, for the vast rates of interest demanded were very difficult for them to meet. But he reached London in a bad time, for the city was swept by the Great Plague and little business could be transacted.

Standish returned in April, 1626, in a fishing vessel to Monhegan, on the Maine coast, and Plymouth sent a shallop thither to fetch him home. He brought with him some sad news for the colonists. The heaviest was that of the death of their beloved pastor, Mr. Robinson, "which struck them with much sorrow and sadness." He had departed this life at Leyden, on the first of March, of "a continuall inward ague." He was, as we already know, buried beneath the ancient Church of Saint Peter, not far from his dwelling. Beside him rest the remains of James Arminius, whose theological tenets lie at the foundation of Methodism. Not only Robinson, but Robert Cushman also, upon whom the colonists had relied for many material things in England, had been taken away by death. The news likewise came by this ship that King James also had passed away and had been succeeded on the throne by his son, who was reigning as Charles I. This boded little good to the colonists, for Archbishop Laud was stretching forth his hand to vex the church. But Charles soon found his realm so infested with the rank growth of Puritanism that he had little time to devote to the insignificant colony which had settled on the coast of New England, behind the long, sandy hook of Cape Cod. Only a few years later, companies of Puritans came flocking to New England, following the lead of the Pilgrims, and one of these we know made its settlement at Massachusetts Bay, where they lived in sweetest amity with their Separatist brethren of Plymouth.

In 1626 one of the chief men of the colony, Isaac Allerton, was sent as a commissioner to England, with instructions to make a composition, upon as favorable terms as possible, with the Company of Merchant Adventurers. The burden of debt to this company was exceedingly heavy, and not only this, but the community system, as we already know, had begun to be very irksome. In the ensuing spring Allerton returned, bringing the draft of an agreement which he had executed with the

Adventurers, subject to the approval of the colonists. By this agreement the Adventurers agreed to accept the sum of eighteen hundred pounds, or nine thousand dollars, in full of all their demands upon the colonists. This would seem to be an enormous sum to be still due to the Adventurers, but the arrangement was "very well liked of and approved by all the plantation." The agreement was accordingly executed. An association was then formed among the colonists, which may perhaps be called a joint stock corporation, by which it was agreed to take over this indebtedness and discharge the colony in its corporate capacity from this incubus. The stock in the corporation was apportioned to the men of the colony, the members to be known as purchasers. It was agreed that the trade of the colony should be in the hands of the purchasers, for the payment of the debt thus assumed.

The colonists now perceived that the community system might be abandoned. The cattle, which had been brought over by Winslow a few years before, had now increased to a considerable herd, and the first movement toward an abandonment of the community system was to make a distribution of these cattle among the families. A small number of goats had also been brought to the colony from Monhegan, and these too were included in the distribution. The cattle were "first equalized for age and goodness and then lotted for, single persons consorting with others, as they thought good." To each family or company of six persons were allotted a cow and two goats. The colonists had also, in some manner which does not quite appear, acquired a number of swine and these were likewise allotted in the same manner.

The colonists now for the first time realized that they might enjoy the felicity of owning their homesteads. The lands of the village were all carefully plotted into homestead lots of twenty acres each and certain men of the colony were appointed to distribute the parcels by lot. The arable lands only were thus allotted, for, since the number of cattle had so increased, they were becoming straitened for pasturage. The meadow lands, therefore, were still retained as common ground, an example followed later by the Puritan settlement at the headwaters of Massachusetts Bay, which was called Boston. And common lands in the latter colony they still remain to this day, and there is no property of which the people of Boston are so jealous as of the lands known as Boston Common, once the common pasture grounds for the cattle of the colony.

The lands of the colony having been allotted, the next charge laid upon the committee of allotment was to set off the dwellings, each to its occupant, for until now all houses had been the common property of the colony. Some of the chief men, as Governor Bradford and Elder Brewster, were allowed to retain their houses without appraisal. All other dwellings and lands were carefully appraised and in the set-off to their occupants he who had a better house was obliged to make an allowance to him who had a poorer. And now that each family in the settlement had its own homestead and its own land for tillage, the colonists had much greater content and the village began to take on a more vigorous and flourishing appearance.

In 1629, so firmly had the colony become settled that they began to discuss the possibility of bringing over the members of the company still remaining in Leyden. This was no slight undertaking. Nine years had now elapsed since the Mayflower had sailed out of the harbor of Southampton. In this period of time we may well suppose that many changes had come to the English colony in Leyden. Some had died, others had grown from youth to maturity, some from England had joined themselves to the colony. There were many, therefore, in Leyden who were entire strangers to them in Plymouth. But all were Christian friends, and as such Plymouth was anxious for a union of interests. And so it was determined to transport to Plymouth the wing of the Pilgrim church which remained in Leyden. It was a difficult and expensive task, for many of the Leyden people were too poor even to procure suitable outfits of clothing for the journey. The party was shipped in two companies. The first of these, comprising thirty-five persons, left Leyden in May, 1629, and arrived in August. The second company left Holland early in March and reached Plymouth in the latter part of May, 1630. The entire cost to the colony of this emigration was about five hundred and fifty pounds, or twenty-seven hundred dollars, including clothing and provisions for the voyage and transportation from Holland to England and thence, in company with a party of Puritan settlers, to Salem. From thence they were brought to Plymouth. In addition to these expenses, the immigrants arrived at a season of the year too late to plant corn for their own harvest, and the colony was obliged to supply them with provisions until the ensuing harvest, in the autumn of 1631. Thus some of these people were dependent upon the colonists for a period of sixteen or eighteen months before they became self-supporting. In the intervening time, to be sure, they had an opportunity to build houses for their own occupancy and to break up the fallow ground for the next spring's planting. This added expense and burden the people of Plymouth took upon themselves without grudging and with the greatest of cheerfulness, "the more," says Bradford, "because the most of them never saw their faces to this day."

It was in the year 1628, it will be remembered, that the first Puritan settlement was founded at Salem, New England. This was followed, in 1630, by the settlement of Boston. When these dates are recalled by the reader it will be readily understood how it was that the Plymouth people took advantage of this new hegira to send for their friends in Leyden.

MYLES STANDISH MONUMENT, DUXBURY

Scarcely two years had passed after the division of the cattle and the disruption of the communal system, when the Plymouth Colony entered fully upon the pastoral stage of development. "For now as their stocks increased and the increase vendible," says Bradford, "there was no longer holding them together, but they must now of necessity go to their great lots; they could not otherwise keep their cattle; and having oxen grown, they must have land for plowing and tillage. And no man now thought he could live except he had cattle and a great deal of ground to keep them, all striving to increase their stocks." Across the bay to the northward were green hill-slopes and rich and abundant pasture lands, and thither the Plymouth colonists turned their eyes. It was a cause of grief to Bradford that the colony, as it seemed to him, began to disintegrate. Especially was he grieved to the heart when Captain Myles Standish, followed soon after by Elder Brewster himself, turned his back upon Plymouth and took up his home upon those alluring hillsides. A new town was presently formed, which was called Duxbury, in remembrance of Duxbury Hall, the ancestral home of the house of Standish in Lancashire. On Captain's Hill in Duxbury to-day stands a noble memorial tower, which perpetuates the name of Standish. In 1666 the son of Myles Standish built a homestead on his father's acres, which stands to-day. So too John Alden and his wife Priscilla made their home in Duxbury, and there, in 1653, their son erected a home, which also stands to the present day. And so Plymouth, having passed through many vicissitudes, entered fully upon an era of expansion.

"Thus out of small beginnings," says Bradford, "greater things have been produced by His hand that made all things of nothing and gives being to all things that are; and as one small candle may light a thousand, so the light here kindled hath shone to many, yea, in some sorte to our whole nation. Let the glorious name of Jehovah have all the praise!"

AMERICA'S CHRISTIAN HERITAGE

"Lastly, (and which was not least,) a great hope & inward zeal they had of laying some good foundation, or at least to make some way therunto, for ye propagation & advancing ye gospell of ye kingdome of Christ in those remote parts of ye world; yea, though they should be but even as stepping-stones unto others for ye performing of so great a work."

GOV. WILLIAM BRADFORD, "Of Plimoth Plantation," 1647

GOVERNOR WILLIAM BRADFORD

William Bradford (1590-1657), second governor of Plymouth Plantation; American historian (author, **"Of Plimoth Plantation"**).

Wm. Bradford was one of the 51 Pilgrim separatists aboard the Mayflower who braved foreboding seas to seek *religious liberty "for himself and his wife and little ones, and for his brethren, to walk with God in a Christian life as the rules and motives of such a life were revealed to him from God's Word."*

A few months after the Pilgrims landed at Provincetown, Bradford was elected governor of New Plymouth colony, a position he held by popular acclaim for 37 years. It was Bradford who had the wisdom to end the communistic system forced upon the Pilgrims by the mercenary shareholders in England. Because of his courage, the fruits of individual enterprise and the right of personal property were restored to the settlers of Plymouth. Bradford wrote a vivid record of the evils and degradations of communism even among people bound together in Christian love and religious enthusiasm.

On November 11, 1620, in the cabin of that tiny Mayflower, anchored off the shore of what is now called Cape Cod, the Pilgrims joined with the other passengers to draw up and sign that historic **Mayflower Compact** - the first civil constitution written on this continent.

Dr. Jordan Fiore reminds us that governments "are developed from an idea - from a concept. The Mayflower Compact was the idea, the concept, that brought forth the government of this nation."

"In ye name of God, Amen ... having undertaken for ye glorie of God and ye advancement of ye Christian faith, and honour of our King and countrie a voyage to plant ye first colonie in ye Northerne parts of Virginia, doe by these presents solemnly and mutualy in ye presence of God and of one another, covenant and combine our selves togeather into a civill body politick ..."[1]

Of those Pilgrims Gov. Bradford wrote, "... *their desires were sett on ye ways of God, & to injoye his ordinances; but they rested on his providence, & knew whom they had beleeved."* Such were the men and women of Plimoth Plantation who brought forth on this continent a new nation dedicated to the advancement of the Kingdom of The Lord Jesus Christ ... *"stepping stones unto others for ye performing of so great a work."*

---

[1]As recorded by Wm. Bradford, History **"Of Plimoth Plantation,"** 1643.
Portrait of Gov. Bradford by John Boatright. Copyright 1986, PRF.

XV

MERRY-MOUNT AND THE
PILGRIMS

WE must now retrace our steps for the
space of a year or two and recall an
episode in Pilgrim annals which has, in its way,
made its impress upon Massachusetts history.
Two of our greatest men in the world of letters
have found in the Pilgrim story the picturesque material for some of their most important works. The "Courtship of Myles Standish" of Longfellow is one of our American
classics, albeit the poet took some liberties, un-
warranted save as poetic license, with facts of
family and of colonial history. And so, too,
Hawthorne, in one of his "Twice-Told Tales"
—the story of "The May-pole of Merry-
Mount"—has set forth, adorned with his rich
exuberance of fancy, the story of Captain
Wollaston and of Thomas Morton, who established upon the rounded hilltop overlooking
Boston Bay, which we to-day know as Mount

Wollaston, an enterprise which caused the good people of Plymouth to join with them of Salem in grieving at the wickedness of humanity. And so, also, Motley, in his forgotten romance of "Merry Mount," turned into charming fiction this picturesquely scandalous occurrence.

It was probably about the year 1625 that a vessel came into Massachusetts Bay bringing a certain Captain Wollaston with a company of followers. Scarcely more than this is known of Wollaston himself, save that he sailed away to the southward after a brief stay in this region. Even the first name of this man is unknown; but the name of Wollaston is perpetuated in a section of the town of Quincy and in the hill which still is known as Mount Wollaston. The locality years ago passed into the possession of John Quincy, for whom the city was named, and from him to a branch of the Adams family, where it still remains. Of Wollaston Charles Francis Adams wrote that he was "a veritable bird of passage, who flitted out from an English obscurity, rested for a brief space upon a hillock on the shore of Boston Bay, giving to it his name as a memorial forever, and then forthwith disappeared into

the oblivion from which he came."[1] Bradford's
record concerning Wollaston is brief. "There
came over one Captain Wollaston," he says, "a
man of pretie parts and with him three or four
more of some eminencie, who brought with
them a great many servants, with provisions
and other implements for to begin a plantation and pitched themselves in a place within
the Massachusetts, which they called, after
their Captain's name, Mount Wollaston."

In Wollaston's company came one Thomas
Morton, with whom we are now chiefly concerned, for Wollaston himself soon sailed away
for Virginia and disappears from history.
Morton seems to have been a London lawyer
of the cheaper sort, much after the manner of
the members of the firm of Quirk, Gammon &
Snap, of Samuel Warren's novel of Ten Thousand a Year, or of Dodson & Fogg in Pick-
wick. Bradford characterizes him as "a kind
of pettifogger of Furnival's Inn," and "a man
having more craft than honestie." Wollaston,
on his departure, left a portion of his company
behind him, under command of one Rassdall;
but Morton usurped his authority and assumed
the control of the colony. The Indian name of

---

[1] Three Episodes of Massachusetts History, I. 162.

the region where this settlement was made was Passonagessit.

There is some reason to believe that this was not Morton's first appearance in New England, but that he was a member of the roystering gang of Wessagusset, which so vexed and troubled the people of Plymouth; and it was perhaps his influence which led to the fitting out of the expedition by Wollaston. No sooner had Morton gained control of the company at Passonagessit than he proceeded to establish a colony upon a unique principle. It has been much the fashion of late years to deride the Pilgrims and Puritans and their austerity and to revile the men who did away with the lively sports of Merry England, of the first James. Truly, the May Festival, as described by some modern writers, was a wholly harmless series of sports, pastimes, and merry-makings, in which innocent young folks adorned themselves with garlands and frolicked and sang about a Maypole. But one has only to look up old Philip Stubbes's Anatomie of Abuses (1583), to learn that the Mayday frolics of Merry England of that period in their manner of conduct differed but little from the Saturnalia of pagan Rome, or the still earlier bacchanalian revels of the primitive Greeks, so hideously set forth by the poet Euripides. Indeed, this period in English history has been called the pagan renaissance. None knew better than the Pilgrims the indecent character of these May revels as practiced in England, and they well knew that, as one writer of that day expressed it, it was "to Satan and the devil that they pay homage and do sacrifice in these abominable pleasures." When, therefore, it became known in Plymouth that Morton and his company had set up a Maypole on the summit of Mount Wollaston and that he had established himself under the title of "Lord of Misrule," after the manner of the English revelers, it is no wonder that the chaste and pious colonists were distressed and horrified. The hill was by Morton renamed Mare Mount, by which we may understand the "Mount of the Sea," or the "Mount of the Merrymakers," as each may prefer to translate the wretched pun. There were no women or girls among the settlers, to add to the merriment of these occasions, and so Morton and his crew summoned to their aid the Indian girls, the "lasses in beaver coats," who joined in the orgies. An abundance of "good liquor" was stored in the log huts, so that drunkenness was added to debauchery and revelry, and license ran high on Merry-Mount.

And now Morton, the leader of the sports, announced himself as a poet. He had not before been known in that character, but now he produced a "poem," which he nailed to the lofty Maypole, and a "songe," which he directed to be sung in a rollicking chorus.[1] In the seventeenth century it was the literary fashion to translate and publish the Greek and Latin classics. Perhaps the first English version of Homer, if we may, possibly, except Chapman's, was brought out by Thomas Hobbes of Malmsbury, the author of the famous Leviathan. Henry Cogan, among other works, produced a translation of Aristotle's Rhetoric and one of the writings of the old historian, Diodorus Siculus. Ovid's Epistles were rendered into English by "several hands," under the direction of Dryden; and Ogilvie brought out a version of Vergil, perhaps the first English translation published. Indeed, there was scarcely a writer of a time prior to the Christian era whose extant works were not translated into English during this

[1] Three Episodes of Massachusetts History, I. 177, 178.

period, and the London bookstalls must have been full of them. Morton had thus an opportunity to acquaint himself, perhaps in a superficial way, with the ancient writings, which were in a measure reflected in the "poem" which he nailed to the Maypole. Evidently, he had some knowledge of the Œdipus Tyrannus of Sophocles, of the third book of the Æneid, and perhaps of some of the tales of Ovid, for his lines, though utterly devoid of sense or meaning, bristled with allusions to the writings of these three worthies. The "songe" was a weak imitation of a Greek epithalamion.

"When the faint echoes of that chorus reached Plymouth," says Mr. Adams, "language in which adequately to express their reprehension of such doings wholly failed the people there."[1] We do not learn, however, that at this time any attempt was made by the Plymouth people to break up this extraordinary colony. But it was not long before Plymouth perceived that the Indians who had beaver skins for sale were more ready to deal with the men of Passonagessit than with them. This puzzle was soon explained, when the horrifying truth burst upon them that Morton was

[1] Ibid., I. 181.

selling guns and ammunition to the natives. No more dangerous practice could be imagined than this, for it was through the exclusive possession of the firearms, of which the Indians stood in terror, that the colonists were able to maintain their superiority over them and enforce peace. Guns in the hands of Indians might easily mean a wiping out of the Plymouth settlement in a night. In short, Morton and his half-dozen companions at Mount Wollaston had not devoted all their time to frivolous pleasures, but, seeing the great pecuniary advantages to be derived from the trade in furs, they had opened up a very lively competition with the Plymouth settlers in that line. In exchange for a gun Morton could obtain a much larger number of beaver and otter skins than by any other form of barter; and when the Indians perceived the vast advantage which the weapon of the white man possessed over their own, they, as Bradford says, "became mad, as it were, after them and would not stick to give any price they could attain to for them, accounting their bows and arrows but as baubles in comparison of them."

Before the close of the year 1627 Plymouth was alarmed to know that not far from one hundred guns were in the hands of the Indians. Some of these had been furnished by English fishermen on the Maine coast, but the majority had been supplied by Morton. Not this alone, but the colonists learned also that the Indians had been furnished with bullet molds and instructed in the method of casting shot of various sizes adapted to the shooting of all varieties of game. They had also been instructed in the composition of gunpowder. The condition was most serious and was so recognized by Plymouth and by the smaller straggling settlements at Piscataqua, at Mishaum, at Winnisimmet, at Thomson's Island, and, a little later, at Salem. The result was a consultation in the interest of safety, by representatives of these settlements, at which it was "agreed by mutual consent to solicit those of Plymouth (who were then of more strength than them all) to join with them to prevent the further growth of this mischief and suppress Morton and his consorts, before they grew to further head and strength."

Remonstrances were first employed with Morton, but to no avail. It was then urged upon him that to sell firearms to the Indians had been expressly forbidden by proclamation by King James. Then cropped out the character of the cheap lawyer, and Morton argued that the proclamation of a monarch, and especially of a dead monarch, bore no penalty and was of no force. To Morton evidently the opportunity for money-making was paramount to any considerations of public safety. The united colonists, now desperate, resolved upon heroic measures and Plymouth was appealed to, to take a bold stand in the matter. In May, 1628, then, Standish and his unconquerable army set out upon a fresh expedition. Learning that Morton was at Wessagusset, Standish proceeded to that settlement and captured him. He escaped from his captors during the night and returned to Mount Wollaston. But they found him in the morning, in his cabin on the hilltop, and laid siege to his stronghold. Morton declared his intention to fight desperately. Summoned to surrender, he answered with "scofes and scorns." But presently he rushed out, apparently with the design of giving battle to his assailants in the open; but he had been drinking heavily, and Standish rushed upon him, knocked up his gun, and arrested him. His captors soon discovered that Morton had loaded and reloaded his gun without once discharging it, until it was filled with powder and shot nearly to the muzzle. It was fortunate for Morton that he, in his drunken frenzy, had omitted the formality of firing his gun.

Morton was taken a prisoner to Plymouth and, by a ship sailing from the Isles of Shoals, he was sent back to England. The little company left at Mount Wollaston evidently continued their scandalous way of life, without further interruption from the Plymouth settlers, for Passonagessit was not regarded by them as within their jurisdiction. Indeed, Standish's expedition had not been undertaken until a definite request to that end had been made by the settlers about Massachusetts Bay. And so matters continued for some months, until Endecott and his company of Puritan settlers crossed the ocean and sat down at Naumkeag (Salem). Endecott, stern old Puritan, then fresh from contact with the English customs of the day, soon heard of the scandalous living at Passonagessit. The place was clearly within the territory covered by the patent granted to the Salem Colony and he took an early opportunity to exorcise the demon. Crossing the bay in an open boat, with a small armed force he scaled Mount Wollaston and—tradition says—with his sword hewed down the Maypole and "rebuked them for their profaneness and admonished them to look there should be better walking."

A year or two later Morton once more appeared in New England and again took up his residence on Mount Wollaston. In the meantime the Winthrop colony had settled on the peninsula of Shawmut, at the headwaters of Massachusetts Bay, and it was not long before they were well informed of the condition of affairs at Mount Wollaston. The first recorded meeting of the magistrates of the Bay colony was held on August 23, 1630. At this meeting it was ordered that Morton, of Mount Wollaston, should be summoned. The next meeting was held on the seventh of September, at which the charges against Morton were heard and discussed. The case was very promptly adjudicated. It was ordered that Morton be placed in the bilbowes (stocks), that he should be deported to England in the ship Gift, then about to sail, that all his goods should be confiscated, and that his house, after the goods should be taken out, should be burned to the ground. And so, when Thomas

MERRY-MOUNT

Morton of Merry-Mount stood upon the deck of the Gift, as she sailed down Boston Bay, he saw the smoke of his burning dwelling ascending to the clouds. He disappeared for some years, but he found a way to revenge himself upon those who had expelled him. He wrote and published a small volume, under the title The New English Canaan, in which he described the country of New England and put his own interpretation upon the character and life of the Pilgrim and Puritan settlers. One of his malicious tales therein told was retold by Samuel Butler, in his Hudibras, first published in 1663. Some years later, while the civil wars were raging in England, Morton once more appeared in New England and walked boldly the streets of Boston. He was seized and confined for a time in jail "for this booke and other things, being grown old in wickedness." And now Thomas Morton disappears from history; but a few scattering copies of his book are still preserved in the great libraries of England and of our country; and he who shall discover in his attic an ancient copy of Morton's New English Canaan will line his pockets with pieces of gold.

XVI

PLYMOUTH'S ERA OF EXPANSION

THE episode of Morton and Merry-Mount may be said to have been the last serious trouble which came upon the people of Plymouth Colony to distress them. Even before this occurrence the crops had begun to meet the demands of the people for sustenance, and from this time forth the struggling colony may be said to have begun to take root and to be firmly established. The colony's trade with the Indians for beaver and otter skins began to flourish, and, although it was somewhat interrupted by Morton's ill conduct, it soon became very valuable. It was still some years before the colony's indebtedness to the Merchant Adventurers was wholly extinguished, but the market for beaver skins was constant, these furs being new to London people, and they rapidly gained popularity. The fisheries also grew constantly in volume and value, so that, all together, the Plymouth colonists ceased to feel an anxiety for the future. The flocks and herds now began to increase rapidly, and with domestic animals attached to every household, the colonists began to seek a wider area.

We have already seen that the increase of their cattle had tempted some to cross the harbor and take up lands for settlement on the rolling hill slopes of Duxbury. The establishment of the Puritan settlement at Boston, in 1630, was also conducive to an increase in Plymouth Colony. The exactions of King Charles and Archbishop Laud led to a great movement of religionists, both Separatists and Puritans, toward New England. In 1628 Laud was made bishop of London and in 1633 he was advanced to the see of Canterbury. During the next decade, or more exactly, between the years 1630 and 1640, no fewer than twenty-six thousand emigrants from England settled in this region. It is probable that by far the greatest number of these immigrants were in sympathy with Puritan ideals and were following the example set by Endecott and Winthrop, who headed this great tidal wave of emigration to New England. There were many, however, who settled within the bounds of Plymouth Colony, and, although there is no means by which the religious tendencies of these may be judged, it is quite fair to assume that the majority were in sympathy with Separatism.

It will be recalled that the patent under which the Leyden Pilgrims designed making a settlement in America carried with it a grant of land in the vicinity of the mouth of the River Hudson. The actual, enforced settlement in New England, then, was in a region to which they had no claim, hence the adoption of the Compact of self-government in Provincetown harbor. With the coming of the ship Fortune, which brought the first addition to their number, an important document was brought to the colony. This was a patent, or charter, for the government of the colony, granted by the Council for New England. It was issued in the name of one John Peirce, "by reason of acquaintance, and some alliance that some of their friends had with him. But his name was only used in trust." The original document, still very legible, is in existence and is preserved with religious care in Pilgrim Hall at Plymouth. A year or two later, when Peirce became assured that the colony would be successful, he, without the knowledge of the colonists, procured another patent to be issued in his own name, by which means he evidently hoped to make the colonists his tenants; "but," says Bradford, "the Lord marvellously crost him," and "with great trouble and loss" they induced Peirce to assign his patent over to the colony.

This second patent, says Bradford, was "of much larger extente" than the first, by which phrase he undoubtedly means that it granted the control of a much larger extent of territory. Its exact bounds cannot be fixed, but evidently it extended northward to meet the southern boundary of the Massachusetts Bay Colony, westward to the waters of the Blackstone (or Seekonk) River, and eastward to include the entire region of Cape Cod.

We have already seen that the settlement of Duxbury was the direct result of the increase of the cattle of the colony, following the abolition of the community system. "Also," says Bradford, "the people of the plantation began to grow in their outward estates, by reason of the flowing of many people into the country, especially into the Bay of the Massachusetts. By which means they were scattered all over the Bay quickly and the towne, in which they lived compactly until now, was left very thin and in a short time almost desolate."

The breaking up and scattering of the original colonists was a source of great regret to Governor Bradford, who not only grieved at the separation of old friends and neighbors, who had suffered and wrought together, but feared perhaps that the consequent weakness might again prove a temptation to the Indians to attack the settlement. Still more greatly was he grieved when the physical division of the colony resulted shortly after in a division of the church, "and those that had lived so long together in Christian and comfortable fellowship must now part and suffer many divisions." It was not long after the settlement had been made at Duxbury that it became a heavy burden, especially for the women and children, to go to Plymouth for public worship and church meetings. "And so they were dismist, though very unwillingly," and a new church was formed at Duxbury.

And now, to prevent, if possible, any further scattering from Plymouth, it was determined to "give out some good farms to special persons that would promise to live in Plymouth and likely to be helpful to the church and commonwealth, and so tye the lands to Plymouth as farmes for the same." In other words, by this plan, those in need of lands for grazing and for cultivation should have these farms allotted to them out of town, which lands should be in charge of hired persons, while the owners should retain their residences in the village. "And so," continues Bradford, "some special lands were granted at a place general called Green's Harbor, where no allotments had been in the former division, a place very well meadowed and fit to keep and rear cattle, good store." But this plan did not prove an entire success, for it soon became evident that the interests of these expansionists lay far more in their farms and cattle yards than in their domiciles in the village. And so, one by one, they broke away from the town influences, "partly by force and partly wearing the rest with importunitie and pleas of necessitie." Governor Bradford greatly bewailed this disintegration of the original Plymouth settlement. "This, I fear," he says, "will be the ruine of New England, at least of the churches of God there and will provoke the Lord's displeasure against them." But the dear man's pessimistic predictions proved without foundation. In 1641 Green's Harbor appears in the list of towns, under the name of Rexame, a name which did not long survive but which was later changed to Marshfield.

These outgrowths from Plymouth marked the beginning of a great era of expansion. The early records of these towns are exceedingly defective, but it is known that it was in 1633 that the settlement pushed out still farther to the northward and formed the town of Scituate. In 1638 a party of colonists came over in the ship Bevis, some of whom settled in the region to the westward of Plymouth, called by the Indians Seekonk. A little later the biblical name of Rehoboth was given to this new settlement, then and now a beautiful agricultural region. Family names of some of these original settlers are still borne by residents of this ancient Pilgrim town. From a part of Rehoboth, locally known as the North Purchase, in 1694, was set off the town of Attleborough. In 1652 still another tract of Plymouth Colony common land was set off, under the name of Dartmouth, out of the bounds of which, in after years, grew the great city of New Bedford. From Dartmouth also has outgrown the town of Westport. In 1639 still another great tract of common land, known as Cohannett, was set off, which later became the city of Taunton. The town of Freetown was in the early days known as Freeman's Land. From this town has outgrown the bustling city of Fall River. In 1656 a part of Duxbury was set off, under the name of Bridgewater, and from this town has outgrown the city of Brockton, surrounded by a halo of vigorous townships.

Very early in the history of Plymouth expansion the movement set in the direction of Cape Cod. The entire cape was common land, claimed by Plymouth by reason of exploration. As early as 1638 the name of Barnstable appears in Old Colony records and from time to time the advancing civilization pushed its way down the narrow cape and out toward the open sea. To-day the automobilist who makes his way in this direction finds a delightfully hard and smooth boulevard connecting a succession of lovely villages and hamlets, like the priceless beads of a jeweled rosary. Latest of all these towns to cease to be held as common land, the property of colony, province, and commonwealth, was Provincetown. For many

years the fishermen of Plymouth made here
their port of call and a little hamlet of
"squatters" grew up upon this common land.
Long years after Plymouth Colony had become merged in the Colony of Massachusetts
Bay, even many years after the colony had
been erected into a royal province, the little
settlement under the far-away sandy hook of
the cape became known as the Province of
Cape Cod; and as the settlement grew larger
and of more importance, it began to be called
Province-Town. But even after a populous
and thriving community had grown up here,
which in the process of time became one of the
greatest whale-fishing ports in all New England, all the real estate in Provincetown was
still common land. Even down to the year
1895, no householder in the town, though his
century-old homestead may have come down
to him from his ancestors, could lay claim to
the land upon which stood his house, save only
through the claim of possession. The fee of
every foot of land within the town of Provincetown, prior to that date, rested in the Commonwealth of Massachusetts, an inheritance
from Plymouth Colony. In that year a legis-
lative act surrendered the State's title to the

PILGRIM MEMORIAL MONUMENT AT PROVINCETOWN

land within the settled limits of the town, thus confirming the titles of the householders; but the region to the north and west of the town was, and still is, reserved to the State as common lands and is known as the Province Lands —the last relic of the once vast public domain of the Old Colony. More than forty Massachusetts cities and towns, comprising a great portion of the counties of Barnstable, Bristol, and Plymouth, have been carved out of the jurisdiction of Plymouth Colony.

By the year 1640 the Colony of Massachusetts Bay had thrown out its boundaries to the southward and presently a disagreement arose among the people of Scituate in Plymouth Colony and of Hingham and Weymouth of the Bay Colony, in regard to the exact boundary line between the two colonies. It is probable that the territories covered by the two charters overlapped each other, with the result that owners of farms upon the border line found it difficult to agree upon the boundaries of their respective holdings. A landowner in the Bay Colony would perhaps drive down his stakes much too far to the south to satisfy his nearest neighbor in Plymouth Colony. The latter would resent the intrusion by pulling up the stakes and throwing them, as far as he found it possible, toward the north. Dwellers in both colonies were equally jealous of what they regarded as their rights, and merrily the battle of words went on, until at length the respective governments were forced to take up the quarrel. Commissioners were appointed to settle the matter, when it was found that, if the boundary line between the two colonies should be drawn in accordance with the terms of the Winthrop patent, it would include practically the whole of the Plymouth town of Scituate. On the other hand, if it were to follow the lines laid down in the Plymouth patent, it would include in Plymouth Colony the Bay town of Hingham. The matter was, however, settled without any serious trouble, and indeed this trifling matter is the only recorded source of friction between the two colonies. The concord and unity between the two are remarkable, when we recall the fact that, in the former days in England, there was as little real sympathy between Separatist and Puritan as between Puritan and Conformist. A persecution common to both seems to have drawn the two wings of Nonconformists together in a mutual bond of sympathy. It is recalled that the route of emigration of the remnant of the Leyden Church to Plymouth was first to Salem, in the company of a party of Puritan settlers. When, soon after the arrival of this party and the removal of the Separatist company to Plymouth, a serious illness broke out among the Salem settlers, Dr. Fuller, the physician of Plymouth, hastened to Salem, where he labored for many weeks, giving the utmost of his skill to the relief of the friends in that settlement. The letter of Governor Endecott conveying his thanks and those of his people for this timely assistance is beautiful in its expressions of brotherly love and affection toward the good friends in Plymouth.

A most charming story, which further sets forth the kindly feeling which existed between the two colonies, is that of a visit paid by Governor Winthrop to his friends in Plymouth. It was nearly two years after the settlement of Boston when Margaret Winthrop, the wife of the governor, joined her husband in the colony. Her arrival was made the occasion of great rejoicing among the colonists and the news of the event soon reached Plymouth. Governor Bradford at once hastened to Boston, to present his congratulations to Governor

Winthrop and his wife. In September, 1632, Winthrop, with a retinue of friends, including the Rev. John Wilson, pastor of the church in Boston, returned this civility. They went by boat to Weymouth and thence proceeded on foot, by the old Indian trail, to Plymouth. The walk at this season of the year, when the country was gorgeous with its ripening glories, must have presented many delights to the party. As the shadows of evening began to fall they reached the outskirts of Plymouth, where they were met by Governor Bradford and his attendants, who had come out from the village to greet the visitors. The story of this visit, which was prolonged for several days, is one of great interest. Especially delightful is the record of the Sunday experiences, of the religious communings which the two governors and their friends held together, and of the manner of their discussions and conversations.

"On the Lord's day," writes Winthrop, "there was a sacrament which they did partake in, and in the afternoon Mr. Roger Williams, (according to their custom) propounded a question, to which the pastor, Mr. Smith spoke briefly; then Mr. Williams prophesied, and after the Governour of Plymouth spake to the question; after him the Elder; then some two or three more of the congregation. Then the Elder desired the Governour of Massachusetts and Mr. Wilson to speak to it, which they did. When this was ended, the Deacon, Mr. Fuller, put the congregation in mind of their duty of contribution. Whereupon the Governour and all the rest went down to the deacon's seat and put into the box and thus returned." [1]

This visit occurred during the brief period which Roger Williams spent at Plymouth, after his first withdrawal from Boston; and this is probably the only occasion on which these four men, illustrious in New England history—William Bradford, John Winthrop, William Brewster, and Roger Williams—were met together.

The settlement of Boston was undoubtedly of vast advantage to the colony of Plymouth. Unlike the Leyden Separatists, many of the Winthrop colonists were men of independent means, and they came abundantly furnished with supplies of every sort, to establish a plantation in comfort to themselves. The contrast

---

[1] Winthrop's Journal, 1, 110.

to the time and manner of the arrival of the Pilgrims was indeed great. They arrived in the height of the summer season, in a fleet of sixteen vessels, bringing with them not only a great supply of provisions, but horses, cattle, fishing gear, firearms and military equipments, and a plentiful supply of clothing. Even some frames of dwellings were among the cargoes. They brought with them also skillful artisans and mechanics, metal workers, salt makers, and other tradespeople, who greatly aided in building up at once a strong and firmly grounded settlement. The new colony was thus not only splendidly equipped, but it was composed chiefly of men of the sturdiest character and of ardent piety, so that they were heartily welcomed by the Plymouth people. Plymouth, with such powerful neighbors as these, was now, even if it had not itself become self-sustaining, placed beyond the danger of distress. It was not long, as we have seen, before the expansion of the two colonies made contiguous their settled limits. New settlements were made later in the Connecticut Valley, at New Haven and at Providence, which were presently united with Plymouth and Massachusetts Bay in a voluntary union.

But in 1692 King James II, of inglorious memory, being upon the throne, a royal province was erected in New England, into which the colonies of Massachusetts Bay and Plymouth were merged, and Plymouth as a separate commonwealth disappears from history.

The true grandeur of the Pilgrims consists in their absolute, unhesitating faith in an overruling Providence, guiding their destiny, but even more in their complete toleration toward the religious beliefs of others. It must be granted that their Puritan neighbors of the Bay Colony, as time went on, were not wholly free from open resentment toward some classes of religionists, whose sentiments differed radically from their own. We can scarcely blame them for their expulsion of Roger Williams, made not so much because he differed with them in religious belief, as that his repeated attacks upon the charter and upon the king's majesty were surely bringing upon themselves the royal displeasure, with a possibility of royal reprisals. But their open attacks upon the Quakers among them are justified by no one of the present day. But against the colonists of Plymouth, none can truly charge that religious oppression or intol-

erance was ever a part of their creed or practice.

"What sought they thus afar?
  Bright jewels of the mine,
The wealth of seas, the spoils of war?
  They sought a faith's pure shrine.
Ay, call it holy ground,
  The soil where first they trod:
They have left unstained what there they found—
  Freedom to worship God."

FOREFATHERS' MONUMENT AT PLYMOUTH

XVII

HOME LIFE IN EARLY PLYMOUTH

WHY the name of Plymouth was chosen for the Pilgrim settlement in New England we have no absolute knowledge. We know that in the year 1614, six years before the arrival of the Mayflower in this region, Captain John Smith, the hero of the Pocahontas incident in Virginia, came to the New England coast upon a voyage of discovery and exploration. In the course of these journeyings he skirted along the shore from Cape Cod to the River Penobscot. He was probably not a skilled geographer, but he made a somewhat crude map of the coast between these points. Later, on a visit to England he displayed this map to the "high and mighty Prince Charles" (later King Charles I), who gave names to "the most remarqueable parts." The result is interesting to us of to-day mainly, perhaps, for the reason that the harbor where was afterward made the Pilgrim settlement appears on this early map as "Plimouth." Nathaniel Morton, in his New England's Memorial, says that the name was given by the Pilgrims, not alone for this reason, "but also because Plimouth in Old England was the last town they left in their native country and for that they received many kindnesses from some Christians there."

Bradford in his history, written probably about the year 1650, in recording the coming of Squanto among them and the treaty with Massasoit, digresses to tell his readers something concerning the previous life of Squanto. Here he records that he was returned to New England by Captain Dermer. In a narrative written by this Dermer, allusion is made to Captain Smith's map, upon which this place is called "Plimouth." It may well be doubted, however, if Bradford in 1620 had seen or even heard of Captain Smith's map; and the choice of the name of Plymouth, in remembrance of their last English port of call, formed probably a happy coincidence. No others of these early names found upon the Smith map have been preserved, save those of Cape Ann and the River Charles, though the names of London,

Edinburgh, Cambridge, and Boston appear upon this map in various localities.

In 1628 occurred an incident the result of which was to hand down to us a description, by a contemporary, of the village of Plymouth in those early days of the colony. This was a visit of a delegation from the Dutch colony on the island of Manhattan, where now is the great city of New York. This party brought with them a letter of greeting and amity from the Dutch colonists, signed by their secretary, Isaak de Rassières. Indeed, Secretary de Rassières was himself a member of the visiting company, for after the return of the party to Manhattan, he wrote a letter to a director of the company in Holland which controlled the plantation. This letter, which was discovered in Holland, in the middle of the last century, gives a description of Plymouth and its people, which is of the greatest interest to us of to-day.

"New Plymouth," writes De Rassières, "lies on the slope of a hill stretching east toward the seacoast, with a broad street about a cannon shot of eight hundred feet long, leading down the hill, with a crossing in the middle, northward to the rivulet and southward to the land. The houses are constructed of hewn planks, with gardens also enclosed behind and at the sides with hewn planks, so that their houses and courtyards are arranged in very good order, with a stockade against a sudden attack; and at the ends of the streets there are three wooden gates. In the center, on the cross street, stands the governor's house, before which is a square enclosure upon which four small cannon are mounted, so as to flank along the streets. Upon the hill they have a large, square house, with a flat roof, made of thick, sawn planks stayed with oak beams, upon the top of which they have six cannon, which shoot iron balls of four and five pounds and command the surrounding country. The lower part they use for their church, where they preach on Sundays and the usual holidays. They assemble by beat of drum, each with his musket or firelock, in front of the captain's door; they have their cloaks on and place themselves in order, three abreast, and are led by a sergeant without beat of drum. Behind comes the governor in a long robe; beside him on the right hand comes the preacher with his cloak on, and on the left hand the captain with his side arms and cloak on and with a small cane in his hand; and so they march in good order and each sets his arms down near him. Thus they are constantly on their guard, night and day."

The original authorities from which alone we are able to learn the story of the Pilgrim life and migration, are concerned chiefly with the politico-religious character of the settlement and settlers. No formal attempt is made, either by Bradford or Winslow, to hand down to us pictures of the home life of these unusual people. Austere we know them to have been, and this characteristic pervaded, doubtless, their home lives and conduct. But here and there in these writings we may, by reading between the lines, or by idealizing some bit of adroit description, draw for ourselves a mental picture of the Pilgrims at their New England firesides. We can readily understand that these people, although tillers of the soil, in their English homes were not, strictly speaking, of the peasant class, for they were close students of the theological problems of the hour and hence were well read on these lines. Before coming to America the Pilgrims had lived for several years under Dutch influences, and these necessarily must have produced an impress upon their characters and customs. It is undoubtedly true, for example, that the custom of holding a festival of rejoicing at the time of the gathering of the harvests—a custom which has brought down to us the most delightful of our New England holidays—was borrowed by the Pilgrim Fathers and Mothers from their friends in the Low Countries.

The earliest dwellings of the Plymouth settlers were, as we know, rudely built of logs, the chinks filled with mud or clay. The roofs were of thatch and the windows, in the absence of glazed sashes, were of oiled paper. They had brought with them no bricks for chimneys, and despite the imaginings of Mrs. Hemans, who believed this to be a "stern and rockbound coast," there is no stone for building to be found on this sandy shore. A hole in the roof, then, could be the only provision for the escape of the smoke from the family fires. Now and then a spark would ignite the thatch of the roof above their heads and for a while the family inhabiting the home, and the entire settlement as well, would be thrown into panic. The first of these serious frights occurred during the epidemic of illness, in the first dreadful winter of the colony. The floor of the common house was strewn with the sick, among whom was William Bradford. Suddenly the roof above them was found to be in flames. The terror of the people, both sick and well, can scarcely be imagined. Not this alone, but those who remained on board the Mayflower, seeing the smoke and flame in the settlement, were filled with the greatest alarm, lest those on shore had been the subjects of an Indian attack. In the absence, then, of stoves, of fireplaces, and even of chimneys, the cookery of the Pilgrims in the early days of the colony must have been of the simplest sort. At that era in the world's history table furnishings, even among the wealthy in England, were not elaborate. Queen Elizabeth never had a fork, and her food was, for the most part, cut apart before being served and eaten with the use of the fingers. We are certain, however, that spoons were in use by the Pilgrims, for a mold for the casting of a spoon brought over in the Mayflower is still preserved. No pottery of any sort, the property of any of the Pilgrim families, has come down to us. In Pilgrim Hall at Plymouth, however, have been preserved an iron dinner pot and a platter of pewter, once the property of Captain Myles Standish.

It is probable that, in common with the masses of the common people of that period, the table-ware of the Pilgrims was of wood.

With the manner of dress of these people we have become somewhat familiar through the portraits of Winslow (the only Pilgrim portrait extant), of Endecott, of Winthrop, of Shakespeare, indeed, and of many others which have been preserved. It was probably the austerity of the Puritans and Separatists which led them to discard the huge ruffs, seen in portraits about the necks of men of the cavalier class, and to substitute the broad white collars of linen. The Holland of the Pilgrim days was famed for its linen industry, and it seems certain that a considerable quantity of this fabric was brought in the Mayflower; and we know that the Dutch visitors brought with them as gifts to the Plymouth colonists, sugar, linen cloth, and "finer and coarser stuffs," by which last expression we may understand fabrics for the making of outer garments. And then, too, Bradford tells us that when, in 1629, the Leyden friends were making their preparations for the voyage to Plymouth, there were required for the outfit of one company one hundred and twenty-five yards of kersey, one hundred and twenty-seven ellons of linen cloth, and sixty-six pairs of shoes. There were also hose, but the stockings of that day were not the knitted garments which we know, but were cut and fashioned of cloth. No doubt a considerable part of the one hundred and twenty-seven ellons of linen cloth was used in the making of the ample white kerchiefs which the Pilgrim women and girls wore about their shoulders. We do not learn that the beaver and otter skins, which were so plentiful in the colony, were used in making garments for the women; but we know that the Indian girls were fond of arraying themselves in coats or jackets of beaver skins, and it is no violent assumption that the Pilgrim women followed their example, especially during the rigorous winters which they encountered.

Neither Bradford nor Winslow tells us of the importation of sheep from England. Yet we find a record of the passage of an act, in 1630, forbidding the sending of any sheep out of the colony. In 1636 an order was adopted by which every householder was obliged, every year, to plant at least one square rod of flax or hemp. Cotton, of course, was unknown in those days. We know that spinning wheels were in use in Holland before their introduction into England and we cannot believe that the industrious Pilgrim housewives neglected their use. It seems more than probable that some of these useful machines were brought in the Mayflower, or at least in the Fortune, or the Anne. Many of the colonists during their life in Holland were engaged in textile industries of various kinds. William Bradford, we know, was a weaver of the coarse fabric called fustian. There were then no mills for these operations, but the work was done largely in the homes of the people. What more probable, then, than that having wool, flax, and hemp at their hands, the sound of the spinning wheel was heard in many Plymouth homes, and that the rude hand looms of Holland were reproduced for the weaving of linen and woolen cloth for the wearing of the people?

Of household furniture the Pilgrims at first had little. We know that many of their goods were in Holland turned into money, which was put into a common fund for the purchase and fitting of the Speedwell. In Pilgrim Hall in Plymouth are a few relics of furniture brought over in the Mayflower—a quaint armchair which belonged to Governor Carver; another the property of Elder Brewster; a carved chest, once the property of Myles Standish; a table, once the property of Governor Winslow, and a cradle, brought over by William White—whose widow married Winslow—and in which no doubt Peregrine White was rocked. There were more than these, perhaps, in the Mayflower's cabin, but further we know nothing. There could not have been a great quantity of furniture stowed in the ship, and during the early days of the colony the furniture of the houses must have been, for the most part, such rudely fashioned articles as they were able themselves to make.

The food of the early settlers was necessarily simple. The supplies brought on the ship in the first voyage were composed chiefly perhaps of salted provisions; for the disease which attacked the company during the first winter was mainly scurvy, a malady produced by eating too freely of salted meats. The Dutch were great lovers of butter, and this at first comprised a considerable portion of their supplies for the voyage. But through the refusal of the Merchant Adventurers to pay over the last installment of money promised for the expenses of the voyage, the colonists were obliged before sailing to sell a quantity of this commodity to obtain funds for the purchase of some more necessary articles. When this was gone they had no more butter until after the arrival of the cattle in the Anne.

Too great stress cannot be laid upon the importance of the discovery of the corn at Cape Cod, for upon this grain, using this for seed, was the chief reliance of the Pilgrims for their food for the first two or three years. From the Indians they soon learned the method of preparing and cooking this grain, which was probably eaten chiefly in the form of "johnny-cake," which, especially in Rhode Island, is a morning dish upon the tables of both rich and poor to this day. The Indians too cultivated beans as well as maize, and from them the Pilgrim women learned to prepare the appetizing dish called by the natives "succotash," a dish which the New England housewife has brought down to us of to-day.

Besides these products of the soil, there were fish in the sea; ducks, geese, and turkeys in the woods; and clams, quahaugs, and lobsters on the shore. By and by, when bricks were brought over from Holland, for the building of some of the lordly mansions of Boston, the

Plymouth settlers built chimneys of brick and reproduced the Dutch ovens, with which they were familiar in the days in Holland. The Pilgrim menu was now greatly enlarged; for with the coming of the cattle they had milk, and there were the eggs of the land and sea birds, so that the New England Indian pudding speedily was invented by these resourceful Plymouth dames and lasses. The Indians had squashes too, which soon found their way into Pilgrim gardens, and now behold the New England pumpkin pie!

Marriages among the Pilgrims were simple ceremonies. Marriage with them, repudiating the Roman idea of a sacrament, was wholly a civil contract, performed by the magistrate, and doubtless Governor Bradford presided at the greater number of the marriages for some years. Who officiated at the marriage of Governor Bradford himself none can say, since he at that time was probably the only magistrate. We have already seen that, after the decimation of the colony by the illness of the first winter, the broken households were speedily repaired by unions with other households similarly bereaved.

We have already seen a picture of Plym-

outh on a Sunday morning, sketched for us by
De Rassières. To the practice of the head of
the household, with his gun, seating himself
at the head of the pew in the meetinghouse,
that he might readily leave in case of an alarm,
may be traced the origin of a similar custom
which prevails to-day—although, it is true, the
fire-arms are now absent. Music in the religious service was not omitted by the Pilgrims,
who, both in Holland and in Plymouth, used
Ainsworth's version of the Psalms. It was
very many years, however, before these austere
religionists permitted the use of the organ in
the service of the church. After the lapse of
some years, it is true, the bass viol was used,
but the unaided voice was, for many years, the
only sound of harmony.

It was a long time before the New England
worshiper suffered his meetinghouse to be artificially warmed. During the bitterest portion
of the Plymouth winter, tiny foot-stoves, holding a handful of glowing coals from the family
hearth, were sometimes smuggled into church
for the use of the women and children, but the
men sturdily refused any warmth save that
which came from the preaching of the Word.
Long years after the settlement of Plymouth,

Judge Samuel Sewall, who attended the Old South Church in Boston, recorded in his diary: "The communion bread was frozen pretty hard and rattled sadly into the plates."

The Plymouth people, we may believe, had little time and little taste for amusements. Labor and worship filled their lives, and sports entered not in. Bradford, however, records the first—and probably the only—instance in which the streets of Old Plymouth resounded with the voice of mirth. In the Fortune, it will be remembered, came several "lusty young men," of whom Bradford says that "many were wild enough." When Christmas day arrived and, as usual in the morning hour, the call was sounded for work, a party of these young men excused themselves to Governor Bradford upon the plea that "it went against their consciences to work on that day." Bradford could not well ignore the claim of conscience, and so his company went away to their day's task, leaving the young men to pass the day as they chose. But when the noon hour came and Bradford and his party returned to the village for dinner, these young men, whose consciences forbade them to work, were found engaged in games in the streets, some playing "stoole-ball," others "pitching the barr." The governor at once "went to them and took away their implements, and told them that it was against his conscience that they should play and others worke." The practice of athletic sports in Plymouth was suspended and we have no record of the time when it was resumed. A recent English writer,[1] in commenting upon this incident, says: "They had set themselves to found a community of saints upon earth, and it was perhaps inevitable that in the program of such high seriousness some things which we now think valuable should have been left out, those fruits of culture and sociability that only a spontaneous joy in living can produce."

[1] Winnifred Cockshott: The Pilgrim Fathers, their Church and Colony, p. 330.

XVIII

THE PLYMOUTH OF TO-DAY

THE oldest of our New England towns in its appearance is typical of all others of its class. The English country village, even of to-day, retains much of the picturesque Elizabethan architecture, the houses with exposed frame of hewn timber, the spaces between filled with plaster or stucco, the roofs long and sloping and covered with thatch. When we for the moment wonder that Englishmen, in transferring their civilization to New England, brought with them no architecture such as this, we remember that in the old home across the sea timber was scarce and could not well be spared, in unlimited amounts, for building purposes. But when the Pilgrims, and later the Puritans, came to these shores they found vast forests, supplying an abundance of lumber. The first, hastily-made dwellings were, as we know, merely log huts. But as the settlement began to expand, more pretentious wooden dwellings took the places of these primitive shelters. Thus, with an abundance of wood for building purposes, a new style of dwelling was evolved, bearing no resemblance to the village architecture of England with which they had been familiar in former days. Hence the villages, which in the lapse of years sprang up all over New England, bore scant likeness to the country village in the homeland. Dwellings sheathed with wood and roofed with shingles of hand-shaved cedar were universal. Beyond doubt, the superiority in comfort of the house of this construction over the rudely built, thatched cottage of England became instantly apparent, hence the typical New England country village.

Such a village we find to-day in modern Plymouth. One may reach the old town from Boston by railway at almost any time of day convenient to the traveler. In the summer season a daily steamboat takes throngs of tourists from Boston and lands them in the town, close by Plymouth Rock. But he who would study well the surpassing beauties of the Pilgrim region, should go by automobile, by way of one of the three or four routes going out of Boston to the southward, any of which will lead to the required goal. Perhaps the most picturesque of these grand highways is the South Shore road, which takes the traveler through Milton, Quincy and Hingham, Scituate and Cohasset, Marshfield and Duxbury, for by this route one catches frequent glimpses of the sea and finds delight in the brilliant masses of flowers with which the roadside dwellers take pleasure in adorning their grounds.

As one enters the outskirts of the Old Colony town, the more modern Plymouth, he is obliged to confess, at first to just a slight feeling of disappointment, for the dwellings are, in many cases, of the very newest sort, and the young roadside trees have not had time to grow to a sufficient size to give character to the place. But as one draws nearer to the older portion of the town, and at last plunges into its very center, a more decided air of mellow quaintness rests upon and about it. Intermingled among the present-day dwellings is seen, now and then, one bearing an air of antiquity and, as the town's center is reached, the square and its outbranching streets take us quickly backward in time, if not to the very Pilgrim days, at least to a time far beyond the ken of any now living.

THE MAYFLOWER PILGRIMS

Are there any dwellings now standing in the old town, is the first thought and query, whose threshold a veritable Pilgrim foot may have trodden? Indeed, they say that there is really one such—the ancient Howland house, built far back in the seventeenth century and many years before the last of the Mayflower Pilgrims was gathered to his fathers. Firm and solid it stands upon its foundations, its great chimney of red Dutch bricks pushing its way through the sharp-pitched roof, the whole wearing an air of old time comfort. And then, too, there is the old Harlow house, with its gambrel roof, built in 1671, its great oak timbers taken from the frame of the first Pilgrim fort and common house, which stood on the hill back of the town, the hospital of the colony during the first terrible winter. Great lindens cast their shade upon the ancient roof in the summer days and a rose vine clambers about the narrow front door and lights up the old dwelling with a wealth of bloom. A row of aged lindens stands also upon North Street, which runs seaward from Town Square and is lined upon either side with mansions of colonial air, glistening in white paint, beautified by Doric columns and porches, and adorned with

THE HOWLAND HOUSE, PLYMOUTH, ERECTED 1667

THE HARLOW HOUSE, PLYMOUTH, BUILT 1671

shining brass knockers and latches upon the doors. Midway of the street is a modern touch amid the quaintness, in the Public Library, built in the refined taste which characterizes so many of our New England public structures of the new day. At the foot of North Street is the shrine of all America—Plymouth Rock, "the corner stone of a nation." Once, many years ago, some patriots whose enthusiasm equaled their poor taste and ill judgment, split off the upper portion of the Rock level with the ground, and dragging it up into the town, deposited it in front of Pilgrim Hall, and surrounded it with an ornamental iron fence. The good judgment of later years compelled its return to its original position, where it was surmounted with a heavy canopy of granite, not so chaste and simple as present-day taste would dictate, but which well expresses the veneration with which the Rock is universally regarded.

Deeply cut into the sloping face of the Rock is the date, 1620, and nothing more. How happy should we feel that the same enthusiasm which cleft the Rock apart and dragged it from its proper restingplace failed to disfigure it with some flamboyant inscription! Just across the street, opposite the Rock, rises abruptly a steep bank, with a plateau above. This is Cole's Hill, on the top of which was the first burial ground of the Pilgrim settlement. Here were buried the fifty and more men and women who fell before the sickle of the grim reaper, during the great sickness which swept the colony, in the first terrible winter. No day of the year, save perhaps in time of storm, is suffered to pass without visits from some modern pilgrims to this sacred shrine. In the summertime, when the stream of visitors is constant, a corps of boys from the Plymouth High School is in constant attendance, to lecture to visitors on the history of the famous Rock. The address delivered evidently has been carefully written by some older person and committed to memory by these bright lads. As an automobile filled with tourists stops by the Rock, one of these boys takes his place close by the shrine, delivers his address and then, if invited, steps into the car and becomes a guide about the town.

Up North Street to the square, and directly on, speeds the car, taking the tourist first, perhaps, to the noble stone church, with its square tower and beautiful windows of stained glass, depicting the chief events of Pilgrim history. The organization of this church is continuous from that of the early church, formed in 1602 in Scrooby. It must be said, however, that in matters of faith this ancient church, for the past hundred years, has wandered far afield from the beliefs of its founders. For two centuries and more the Pilgrim church retained the faith of the fathers in the divinity of Christ. But when, about the year 1812, over our country swept a great revolt against the truthful doctrines of Calvinism, its influence was strongly felt in Plymouth as elsewhere. The Pilgrim church, we remember, in Scrooby and in Leyden never adhered closely to the Calvinistic doctrine of predestination; but in the revolt against "orthodoxy," this church with others was swept along with the tide until it plunged into Unitarianism. There were some who quailed at the thought of forcing the old historic church from the faith in which its founders, two centuries before, had firmly planted it; but they were too few in numbers to be able to stem the current, so they broke away and formed a new organization, while those who believed themselves reformers retained control of the early formation. They who kept pure the ancient Pilgrim faith built a new church edifice across the way, and have there upheld the old traditions. Some years ago the building of the first church was destroyed by fire, and upon its site was erected the present beautiful edifice.

Upon the hill which rises abruptly back of the church is the burying ground, where many of the "forefathers of the hamlet sleep." Here is identified the spot where lies John Howland, one of the Mayflower company, and close by a tiny column marks the probable resting place of Governor William Bradford. Across the bay in Duxbury is to be seen the grave of Myles Standish, guarded by antique cannon. But of the Mayflower company the resting places of these alone can be identified.

From Burial Hill the visitor will turn his steps to Pilgrim Hall, in form a little Doric Greek temple, where are sacredly preserved many undoubted relics of Pilgrim days and people. Some of these were mentioned in a previous chapter. None of these relics is of greater interest than the old black-letter Geneva Bible once owned and studied by William Bradford. His second wife, Alice Carpenter, too, had held it in her hand, for upon the margin of a leaf is seen her family name, traced in a delicate handwriting. Preserved here with the most sacred care is also the ancient charter, held by the Pilgrim Society in such reverence that never has a photographic copy been allowed to be made. Here too is the original portrait of Governor Edward Winslow, painted in England on the occasion of one of his visits to the old home, made in behalf of the colony. This is the only known portrait of any of the Pilgrim company. Here are also other paintings, modern but scarcely less famous—Lucy's great picture of the "Departure from Delfthaven," Sargent's picture of the "Landing," and Weir's familiar "Embarkation." The sword which Myles Standish girt upon his thigh when he took up his memorable marches lies in a glass case, beside other relics. It was old, they say, even when Standish owned it; for, says tradition, it was an inheritance to him from a Crusader. Upon its blade is seen a curious inscription in Arabic, which has been but partially deciphered:

"Spake in the pride of his heart, Myles Standish, the captain of Plymouth,
'This is the sword of Damascus I fought with in Flanders.'"

THE MAYFLOWER PILGRIMS

What two relics of Pilgrim history can be of deeper, more thrilling interest than the Bible of Bradford and the sword of Standish? But there are many lesser relics here, so that one may pass many hours with profit and pleasure in this hall. Here is the cradle in which was rocked the first white child born in New England, Peregrine White, who first saw the light of day in the cabin of the Mayflower, as she lay in Provincetown harbor. Here is the candlestick from whence was cast, through the cabin windows of the Mayflower, "a pale, yellow gleam upon the water," that little light which has "streamed forth now broad and brilliant, across three hundred years, passing over continent and ocean and shining with the clear radiance which all men can see and understand."

"How far that little candle throws its beams!"[1]

Here too are some ancient yellow bricks, worn thin by the tread of many feet which have crossed the wharf in Delfthaven, whence sailed the Speedwell with the Leyden Pilgrims. A century, two centuries, three mayhap, these

---

[1] Henry Cabot Lodge at the dedication of the Pilgrim Monument at Provincetown, August, 1910.

FROM THE DAYS OF LONG AGO

Top—Elder Brewster's Chair and the
Cradle of Peregrine White

Middle—Sword, Pot, and Platter of
Myles Standish

Lower—Ancient Spinning-Wheel and
Governor Carver's Chair

bricks formed a part of the pavement of the old wharf, and one likes to think that it is in no way wholly impossible that they are ancient enough to have felt the pressure of the feet of Bradford, and Brewster, and Robinson.

Other Pilgrim traces are to be found in modern Plymouth. When the "meersteads" were laid out and were granted to the families by lot, the rear line of each bordered upon the brook. These original "meersteads" have been preserved as at the beginning, having been passed down from owner to owner through the three centuries which have passed. The log-houses, their first dwellings, of course long ago disappeared, and modern structures have taken their places; but the original lines of the lots have been preserved, sharply sloping downward to the brook and made picturesque by long lines of wooden steps to give easy access to the stream. It is probable that such steps have been maintained on these slopes from the beginning and that the housewives by this means obtained their supplies of water.

The Town Brook too, one of the chief features of the early settlement of the colony, still flows from Billington Sea to the bay. About the name of this "sea" hangs a story. The exploits of young John Billington, first in exploding his father's gun in the Mayflower's cabin and later of losing himself in the woods, have been narrated. He was undoubtedly a somewhat stupid boy; but he had a brother, named Francis, who was evidently possessed of keener wits. For one day Francis became lost in the woods, but instead of wandering about for days and feeding on berries, he climbed a tree and made a reconnoissance. He not only discovered his own whereabouts, but discovered also a large pond, or inland sea, which proved to be the source of Town Brook. The report of this discovery created a profound interest in the colony, and the sheet of water, in the lad's honor, was called Billington Sea, a name which it has since borne. A picturesque sheet of water it is, for civilization has not ruined its natural beauties, and the people who now abide in Plymouth, some of whom have no difficulty in tracing their lineage from men or women of the Mayflower company, are proud of this feature of the old town's landscape. The Town Brook pours its stream downward as gently as it did three centuries ago. Along its banks, in some places it is true, the hand of man has pushed aside the

PILGRIM MEERSTEADS, PLYMOUTH

AN INTERIOR VIEW OF PILGRIM HALL, PLYMOUTH

picturesque, to make way for the realities of practical affairs; but the place is still to be seen where Winslow fearlessly descended the slope, crossed the brook, and advanced up the slope of the opposite hill to meet and parley with King Massasoit. A beautiful stream too is Eel River, closely overhung with drooping branches of trees, forming a grateful shade. And he who sits beneath these trees and gazes upon the placid water may perchance call up vision of Squanto, the Pilgrim settlers' friend, standing waist deep in the flood, and with naked feet treading out the eels. With his hands he draws them from their oozy beds and so does his humble part to the support of his white friends.

And so they who frequent the Old Colony town are able to point out to the stranger and the traveler very many such delightsome spots, preserved by nature in much of their pristine beauty. But the Indian trails, leading to Boston and elsewhere, have long ago become overgrown and have become disused as advancing civilization has crowded them aside, though traces of these trails are even now seen here and there by the cross-country pedestrian. But long since the bridle path and the cart path took the place of the foot trail; the turn-pike succeeded the cart path; and now the hard and smooth automobile highway penetrates every part of the Pilgrim country. From the center of Plymouth southward runs perhaps the finest of these highways, stretching itself away for a hundred miles, in a mighty curve through the great bending Cape and joining the Old Colony town to its offspring at the Cape's uttermost tip.

It is an unmatched story which we have told, a story of hardships and distresses, of trials and tribulations of every sort; of unbounded, unflinching faith; of glorious triumph at the last. Some of the men and women of the Mayflower were spared to enter fully into the promised land; but even those of the mightiest faith could scarcely have pictured to themselves a great nation, yea, a world, in which their tenet of freedom of worship should be the chief corner stone.

INDEX

Notes

Notes

Notes